Brandon,

Welcome to this amazing
to have you on the team. Thank you for being
part of this dream!

THE MILLENNIAL **CEO**

GETTING SH*T DONE!

RICK A. HAMMELL

THE MILLENNIAL **CEO**

GETTING SH*T DONE!

ForbesBooks

Published by ForbesBooks, Charleston, South Carolina.
Member of Advantage Media Group.

ForbesBooks is a registered trademark, and the ForbesBooks colophon is a trademark of Forbes Media, LLC.

Printed in the United States of America.

10 9 8 7 6 5 4 3 2 1

ISBN: 978-1-950863-70-9
LCCN: 2021916422

Layout design by Mary Hamilton.

This custom publication is intended to provide accurate information and the opinions of the author in regard to the subject matter covered. It is sold with the understanding that the publisher, Advantage|ForbesBooks, is not engaged in rendering legal, financial, or professional services of any kind. If legal advice or other expert assistance is required, the reader is advised to seek the services of a competent professional.

Advantage Media Group is proud to be a part of the Tree Neutral® program. Tree Neutral offsets the number of trees consumed in the production and printing of this book by taking proactive steps such as planting trees in direct proportion to the number of trees used to print books. To learn more about Tree Neutral, please visit **www.treeneutral.com**.

Since 1917, Forbes has remained steadfast in its mission to serve as the defining voice of entrepreneurial capitalism. ForbesBooks, launched in 2016 through a partnership with Advantage Media Group, furthers that aim by helping business and thought leaders bring their stories, passion, and knowledge to the forefront in custom books. Opinions expressed by ForbesBooks authors are their own. To be considered for publication, please visit **www.forbesbooks.com**.

I would like to dedicate this book to all of my champions and cheerleaders throughout my life, from family to friends and colleagues. Most importantly to the late Rubye Slater-Harmon, and to Henry Hammell Sr., Andrea Hammell, Sheriah Hammell, Kelly Thornton, Major Hammell, Tara Coatie Singleton, Dario Gonzalez, Michael Bercovich, and all of my current and former employees of Elements Global Services. If it wasn't for each of you, I wouldn't be who I am today. From the bottom of my heart, thank you!

CONTENTS

CHAPTER ONE

HOW IT BEGAN

I was just nineteen at the time, but the words on the computer screen were still far from the worst that had ever been said to or about me in my life. "This is going to *destroy* him," the email began. What followed was a plot devised by my manager to have me terminated from my position as a front desk manager for a major hotel chain. She had been angry with me for weeks, after I disclosed to her bosses information that she had wanted to keep hidden. She had apparently been scheming to get me fired ever since, evidenced by the plan she had written out in great detail and sent to a coworker. If only she had not mistakenly left the email open on the computer we all had to share, her plan might have worked. The thought of how close I'd come to being thrown out on my own with no job or support was terrifying, but it wasn't only the deceptive nature with which she had planned to "destroy" me that concerned me so much. What triggered my survival instincts most of all was the fact that this wasn't the first time I'd been betrayed by someone with authority over me.

The decision to quit my job came swiftly. Days after discovering her email and before I had another job lined up, I submitted a three-week resignation notice. I knew the environment was too toxic and volatile to be repaired quickly, and even if it could be, the organization offered little to no protection or resources to its employees who spoke out against mistreatment from their superiors. In hindsight, the incident was the kick start I needed to find my way into the human resources world.

I dedicated myself to learning everything I could about workers' rights, not only to help protect myself from workplace mistreatment but also so I could help others who were experiencing the same or worse conditions in their jobs. I knew at the time what most workers know: that the role of HR is to protect both the company and the employees. I would learn later that the most effective way to execute that role is for HR to ensure that the company doesn't hurt itself by committing wrongs against its employees. My employer had failed to protect me, but they had also failed to protect themselves. They lost a valuable employee, but had I chosen to pursue them, they had opened themselves up to legal vulnerabilities as well.

Unfortunately for me and fortunately for them, the bills weren't going to pay themselves, and I committed all of my time and energy toward finding another job while I considered a new career trajectory. Call it luck, fate, or pure coincidence, but after applying to a number of jobs, I received an offer from a technology company in need of an office manager who would also serve an HR function at their Atlanta office. In the beginning, I had no idea what I had gotten myself into, but I was fortunate to have a phenomenal mentor named Crystal Brooks, who taught me nearly everything there was to know about human resources and helped me navigate my new career path. Through Crystal I learned not only the day-to-day duties of HR work but the purpose of it as well. I was able to connect the human element of HR's role to organizational management innovations (e.g., culture, office design and layout, communication protocols, talent recruitment, development, retention) to business solutions that benefit the company (e.g., legal liabilities, cost efficiency, human capital). Eight years later, that path led me to a position as vice president of HR with a government contracting firm, before I founded my own HR technology and services company.

The journey from front desk manager at a hotel to the CEO of an international company was not a straightforward path; nor was it an easy one. I have endured, and still endure, countless moments of self-doubt, prejudice, and a line of "failures" as I worked to build my own business from scratch. But humility—the ability to see other people and events as being just as important as you are—has been a guiding principle in my life ever since I was a teenager.

I learned about true humility through a series of trials and tribulations, which ultimately taught me that I would have to work harder than most to get what I wanted. I also gained a depth of empathy for others that I never would have understood had I not been humbled by the challenges with which I was forced to grapple. In hindsight, the humility that flourished in the wake of my adversities has served as the backbone for some of my proudest accomplishments and decisions, but such a realization does not come easily.

As a CEO and entrepreneur with more than two hundred employees, with fifteen global regional offices supporting clients in more than 135 countries, I know now that you can build the highest level of authenticity simply by listening to others. How much authenticity you build as a leader depends on how successful you are in processing their feedback and finding a way to understand it, as well as how diligent you are in improving your weakest leadership qualities. People don't expect a good or even great leader to be perfect, but they do expect them to be considerate enough to hear the concerns of others, humble enough to acknowledge their own faults, and strong enough to work hard toward becoming a better leader and person.

> **PEOPLE DON'T EXPECT A GOOD OR EVEN GREAT LEADER TO BE PERFECT, BUT THEY DO EXPECT THEM TO BE CONSIDERATE ENOUGH TO HEAR THE CONCERNS OF OTHERS, HUMBLE ENOUGH TO ACKNOWLEDGE THEIR OWN FAULTS, AND STRONG ENOUGH TO WORK HARD TOWARD BECOMING A BETTER LEADER AND PERSON.**

Connecting with your own definition of humility and how to apply it to your leadership skills begins by reflecting on the hardships you have faced in your life, particularly those that humbled you in the first place. Allowing yourself to feel those experiences fully is the best way to put them to productive use now, all of which I had to learn during this journey.

BREAKDOWN, BREAK UP, BREAK OUT

The day my father found out that I was gay was the same day I came out to my entire high school. I was fifteen, and the day before the "big one," I had been sitting in English class at my suburban Chicago high school when my teacher—a kind woman who encouraged open and honest communication in the classroom—began a conversation on how words can hurt us. In what now feels like a blur, the conversation turned to gay people and their experiences in society. Teenagers being teenagers, my classmates quickly let the homophobic slurs fly before one student declared, "They should be killed!" While the class roared in amused agreement, I saw my friend—and one of only a few who knew that I was gay at the time—staring at me with a look that said, "You should say something." Our classroom had essentially morphed into an impromptu hate rally, and I had no interest in testing the seriousness of their claims. "*No*," I mouthed to her while slowly shaking my head.

The gravity of the events that day didn't fully sink in until late that afternoon when I was alone in my bedroom. I had time to process just how disgusting and terrifying their words had actually been. The longer I thought about it, the more upset I became. Poetry had become a favorite form of escape for me at the time, so I retrieved my notebook and wrote a poem I titled "Take a Walk in My Shoes." I wrote the poem not only to those classmates but to anyone else who shared similar views. I told them that the only thing different about me was that I was gay. I asked them how they could call themselves Christian, Muslim, Jewish, or simply a decent human being and yet hate me just for being who I am. I asked them to imagine a life in which every morning they wake up and, for at least one moment, feel unloved by everyone in the world.

The next day I handed that poem to my English teacher and told her that I would like her to read it to the class, under the condition that she would not tell anyone who had written it. I needed my classmates to know how hurtful and dangerous their words were, not just to me but to all gay people everywhere. She agreed and read it to the class, breaking down in tears halfway through the piece. After class, she asked me if she could share it with the dean. I told her she could, and before I knew it, I was sitting in the dean's office watching tears stream down both her and my English teacher's faces.

"Rick, we have an assembly this afternoon called Names Really

Hurt Us, and I would love for you to speak at it—maybe read your poem to the school."

My eyes widened in disbelief, and the words couldn't have shot out of my mouth any faster: "Nope, nope, nope. That is *not* happening. No way."

The dean was convincing, though, telling me that since I was somewhat popular and had written such a moving poem on the subject of bullying and bigotry, I was in a unique position to help other students who might be in the same situation but who were less comfortable or capable of expressing those feelings. After some careful consideration, I agreed to do it because I saw it as an opportunity to stand up for others.

A few hours later, I found myself standing at a podium on stage in front of an auditorium filled with my peers. I took the biggest breath of my life and somehow managed to get through the entire poem without fainting.

When I finished, I'm certain you could hear a pin drop. I looked up from the page and out into the crowd to see several students crying, some clapping, and, unsurprisingly perhaps, most of the guys wearing expressions of shock, ridicule, or some confused combination of the two on their faces.

I was in shock, too, with few ideas about what I had just done and even fewer about how it might shape my life. By the end of the day, a lot of my male friends had stopped talking to me, each one seemingly replaced instantly with a new female friend. In less than five minutes, my social circle and the rest of my high school experience had completely and irrevocably shifted.

Owing to his close relationships with a lot of people at my school, word of my spontaneous poetry reading traveled quickly to my father. It took longer than five minutes, but the words between us soon boiled over into the room late that same night. The arguments escalated in their capacity to inflict pain over the course of a week or so before culminating in my father telling me that I was a curse from God and had to leave his house and reminding me I that was going to fail without him.

Defiant and devastated, I stuffed a few trash bags full of clothes, called a friend for a ride, and stormed out of the front door, vowing never to return.

Growing up, my father was my hero. He was a successful businessman who spoiled my siblings and me rotten with gifts and trips, always ensuring that we had a nice home in a nice neighborhood and a quality education. He had always been strict and demanding of us, but I never could have imagined him throwing me out for any reason, let alone because I found the courage to be honest about who I am.

I'm now roughly the same age as my father when he learned that his firstborn child is gay, and though I don't agree with his reaction, I have a better understanding of it today than I did then. I know he was scared, confused, and even hurt to finally hear what he had known all along. He was from a different generation, raised with different norms and roles in society than the ones I had experienced. I know now that he worried how he could relate to me, how we could ever understand each other. He snapped under the weight of all those fears and questions, but his pride wouldn't let him acknowledge it. I didn't have those insights at the time, of course. I only knew that he wanted me out of his house.

I was still in shock when I heard my friend's voice. "Rick? Rick, where do you want me to take you?" We had been driving for a few minutes, but I hadn't thought about what was next, only what I had lost in a single day. I was in love, at least as much as a fifteen-year-old can imagine love, with a boy a few years older than me at the time, and I knew he would soon be getting off from his shift at the local Blockbuster (remember those?). I was sure that he would help me, so it was another breathtaking blow when he told me that I couldn't stay with him.

As the betrayals piled up, I decided to go to my stepmother's mother's house and ask if I could stay with her temporarily since she lived nearby. "You can sleep on the couch," she said, "but only for five days."

I felt like I was being rejected by every person I'd believed I could depend on most, all within a matter of hours. Exhausted and increasingly desperate, I asked a friend named David if I could stay with him and his mother for a while. David and his mother were sympathetic to my situation and took me into their home, where I stayed for roughly a month while I looked for work and a place of my own.

Until that night, I had never had to think about money or a job. If you've ever seen the movie *Mean Girls*, my life was like that of "the Plastics" clique: popular, affluent, well dressed, and pampered. Of course, being Black and gay came with more challenges than most of my peers, and my father and I had had a somewhat contentious relationship for a few years prior to our estrangement, but I had enjoyed many of the privileges that come with an upper-middle-class life in Evanston, Illinois. I went to a great school and lived in a safe and mostly progressive neighborhood, and if I asked him, my father was almost always willing to give me money with few or no questions asked. Once, when he reminded me that money didn't grow on trees, I sarcastically replied, "It's paper, so actually it does." I was *that* kid, spoiled and sassy and thought he knew it all. And for a while, I did. Before I was truly aware of the myriad struggles that came with my identity, I believed that I would have an easy road to any dream I wanted. Now I found myself sleeping on my friend's mom's couch with everything I could call my own in two trash bags on the floor and no money whatsoever.

I didn't have time to dwell on the other things I'd lost: those dozens of friends at school, the boy who I thought loved me, my home, my pampered lifestyle, and even my father to some degree. I needed to figure out how I was literally going to survive before I could sort through that chest of trauma and sorrow.

If anyone had ever been humbled more swiftly, fallen from their high horse to a pit of rejection and anxiety in more dramatic fashion, then I had not met them. Would I trade that humility for never having to experience such pain? Never. Would I do anything differently knowing what I know now? Absolutely not. I had never been prouder of myself. For the first time in my life, I knew who my authentic self was, and I had chosen to fight for that truth no matter what consequences might follow. I felt as though I had exhaled for the first time in my life. It was also the first time in my life that I went to sleep without any idea of what the rest of my life would be like, but I wasn't especially scared of the future either. It was all mine now, and I was free to do with it whatever I wanted—a liberty that for a fifteen-year-old kid in the city with nowhere to go and no one to answer to is akin to walking a tightrope.

In retrospect, as much as my leaving home had to do with bettering myself, I didn't know that at the time. I found direction and comfort in helping others take their own leap of faith, encouraging them through my actions to put down whatever guards they had raised in the face of their adversities and see the possibilities of a happier, freer life. I wanted to show them that it was possible to overcome hardships, to learn to let go and trust themselves.

I was determined to give them, and myself, a story of triumph rather than of trials, tribulations, and tragedy, one that could not just inspire people but that could also save lives. I became the first guy at my high school to bring a male partner to prom. I still played soccer. I still hit home runs in baseball games. And a few guys even got beat up by a "f****t."

Of course, I had no intentions to write a book at the time. My story of beating the odds was still being written, after all. But after having the worst day of my life, I committed myself to proving everyone wrong who had rejected me and told me that I would fail, my father most of all. Once I did, opportunities for work, friendship, love, education, and a career began to present themselves to me. I needed humility and honesty in my life to see and appreciate those opportunities, but I never took any chance to improve my life for granted ever again.

I WAS DETERMINED TO GIVE THEM, AND MYSELF, A STORY OF TRIUMPH RATHER THAN OF TRIALS, TRIBULATIONS, AND TRAGEDY, ONE THAT COULD NOT JUST INSPIRE PEOPLE BUT THAT COULD ALSO SAVE LIVES.

Through sharing my story of adversity with others, I realized that my struggles speak to a much larger audience than I had ever expected to reach, as everyone has made mistakes, suffered losses, had their hearts broken, and even been neglected and/or abandoned in some way, shape, or form in life. Everyone finds inspiration in a story of never bowing down to whatever difficulties lie before you, but my story is only one of millions of similar experiences. I still grapple with these circumstances every day, but I've grown so much stronger and determined by being myself and knowing my purpose. I would have never been able to build and lead a successful international company with more than two hundred employees worldwide if I had not learned the humility and empathy of losing everything and being forced to fend for myself at a young age. If what you stand to gain is greater than what you stand to lose, then take the risk and go for it. Humility will serve as your greatest compass, your truest North Star, and I'll prove that idea to you in the chapters to come.

CHAPTER TWO

PATIENCE

When I put in my notice of resignation at my hotel job, I had no idea what I was going to do next. I had moved to Atlanta less than a year prior after the hotel chain offered me a promotion, and I still hadn't made many contacts or friends who might have been able to help me find another job. But my grandmother had grown up in Georgia, and after I moved to Atlanta, we always joked that we were the last Georgia peaches in the family. Her father had owned several businesses in their small town, a feat that had put her and her family in the crosshairs of the Ku Klux Klan, a powerful and seemingly omnipresent terrorist group that would eventually murder three of her brothers. She was among the few Black women fortunate enough to attend Atlanta's Spelman College during the 1940s and '50s, and it was during that time that she met my grandfather while he was attending nearby Morehouse College. Shortly after completing her studies at Spelman, my grandmother moved to Chicago and began a family of her own.

Upon my moving to Atlanta, she was the person I called nearly every day. She was my rock, my source of love and encouragement, which is something I believe we all need in our lives, especially when we find ourselves in difficult times.

So when I left the hotel, I thought of my grandmother urging me to always be patient and grateful. I admired her for her display of strength and compassion, her work ethic, and her nurturing character. I'm as sure that she influenced my decision to stand up for myself and seek out another job as I am that she inspired my choice to pursue HR as a career. She helped me see that I had faced enough adversity in my life to know that I could take a leap of faith on myself and find a solution before I smacked face-first into the concrete.

Patience, like most virtues, is much easier said than done. If you look up the word *patience* in the dictionary, you will find it defined as "the capacity to accept or tolerate delay, trouble, or suffering without getting angry or upset" or a similar description. That's a difficult disposition to maintain for anyone at any age, but it's a particularly hard trait to master if you have less experience with things not going your way.

Millennials, myself included, and the incoming Gen Z generation often find themselves at something of an existential crossroads, teetering between the optimism, exuberance, and the impatience of youth with the more realistic, conventional, and tempered nature of veteran adulthood. What I have learned so far is that we need to foster patience within ourselves by not only consistently reminding ourselves of its importance but also by holding ourselves accountable to it.

For me, the key to empowering a more patient mindset has been to anticipate—and accept—a certain degree of disappointment, failure, setbacks, and general challenges in everything I do. That isn't to say that you should expect to fail at whatever you set out to accomplish; rather, you shouldn't be blindsided by things going wrong—like when I had to make the choice to resign from the hotel without another job lined up—or by things moving slower than you'd hoped they would.

No matter what you choose to do with your life, you will have obstacles large and small, and some will have more than others. But as an entrepreneur or business leader, you cannot accept defeat the moment your plans begin to stumble. Developing stronger patience and humility, though, will help you to maintain the kind of calm and mental clarity you need for successful problem-solving.

Humility and patience are intertwined, each depending on the other to reveal their individual benefits. You cannot understand, much less utilize, patience without being humble. Knowing that you are vulnerable and that you are *not* all knowing all the time is critical to one's ability to see and understand the myriad solutions to a problem. Patience is not the art of waiting for someone else to find a solution for you. It is the ability to survey a problem, design a plan to resolve it, and then allow enough time for the solution to play out. Patience is a game of nerves, and fostering less hubris and entitlement within yourself is key to mastering it.

PATIENCE IS A GAME OF NERVES, AND FOSTERING LESS HUBRIS AND ENTITLEMENT WITHIN YOURSELF IS KEY TO MASTERING IT.

There is a degree of convenience at our fingertips twenty-four hours a day that can challenge our commitment to patience in many ways, though. Along with the changes to how we work and interact, technology and the internet have made it easier and faster to do everyday tasks, from banking to socializing to shopping and more. And while we can order dinner through an app and have it delivered in a matter of minutes without seeing or even speaking to another person, that level of immediacy isn't really how life works.

That once barren virtual space that is the internet is now among the hardiest manifestations of progress and change modern civilization has ever seen, offering much of its contribution as a platform for further collaborative innovations. Progress begets progress, you might say. But running a business requires a lot of patience and interaction with your staff and customers every day. You can't automate human interaction and performance. Too often, we want to wave a magic wand and turn employees into the employees we believe they should be. But if you're a real manager, it's like raising a plant from a seedling. If you want them to become a flower, you have to nurture them and give them life, which takes patience because that process takes time. There is no button you can push to get there instantly.

The foundation of our work in HR is likewise built around the need for patience. The ability to understand and empathize with the experiences of others depends on one's level of patience to listen, learn, and adapt. When I founded my business, my relationship with patience had to evolve to accommodate my new responsibilities as a leader. I knew that no one would be as passionate as I am about my own business, but if you're paying someone well to do a job and they don't do it correctly, then you're tempted to lose your grip on patience.

Imagine that you paid someone to clean 100 percent of your house and later found that they had only cleaned 80 percent of it. You might ask for 20 percent of your money back and never hire them again, right? Or you might try a different approach and talk to them about why they didn't clean the whole house. If they have a good explanation, then you'll likely give them another opportunity. That moment of patience gives you the clarity to ask the right questions and reach the source of any discrepancies in your expectations. That's why patience is such a critical skill to master as a business leader, because it's rare for anyone to do their job exactly like you want them to all the time. Having enough humility to consider that maybe you didn't communicate yourself very well or understanding that people simply make mistakes at times aids a better response to conflict when patience is needed most.

The best business leaders are able to figure out how they can build the best company from the inside out. Part of that equation is making sure that your company is a great employer, one that's capable of creating and maintaining a productive and happy staff (e.g., offers good pay and benefits, prioritizes a healthy workplace culture, expresses gratitude to workers). We expect that by being a great employer, every employee will be great in return, but it's not always such an ideal two-way street. To a certain extent, employees are always going to feel that their employer owes them more, especially if they aren't passionate about their work. Almost by design, someone working a full-time job they don't enjoy is going to want more money to compensate for their unhappiness in that position. Finding out why a worker is unhappy and strategizing a way to help them become more engaged in their work is a major part of any HR department's responsibilities, and patience is the backbone of such a function.

How well you work with different personalities is essential not only to business leadership but to life in general. You must, at times, be a chameleon to improve your communication with others. Truly listening to and understanding other people's ideas rather than

HOW WELL YOU WORK WITH DIFFERENT PERSONALITIES IS ESSENTIAL NOT ONLY TO BUSINESS LEADERSHIP BUT TO LIFE IN GENERAL.

shutting everyone else out and solely following your own ideas is a basic requirement for healthy relationships in all areas of one's life. People are going to make mistakes, and you may even be able to do something better than they can, but they have to learn as well. Having the patience to let them make mistakes is great, but the patience to help them learn from those mistakes and improve is the mark of strong leadership.

A great leader recognizes one's potential rather than their flaws and weaknesses alone. My grandmother saw my potential before anyone else did, including myself, and she never let me wallow in my mistakes nor the wrongdoings of others. It takes patience to realize your own potential, too, but having someone in your corner who helps you see your worth and encourages your personal growth makes the process much less daunting. A great leader serves as a mentor to their people in that way, leading with patience and humility to empower the potential of those around them.

CHAPTER THREE

POTENTIAL

Before I launched my company Elements Global Services, I experimented with entrepreneurship through a catering business that I dubbed the Windy Peach, a name meant to honor my Chicago roots as well as my grandmother's home state and the state of my residence at the time, Georgia. After leaving my job at the hotel and joining the HR department for a government contracting firm just outside of Atlanta, I decided to pursue something entrepreneurial on the side to test whether I could ever see myself running a business as a full-time career. A catering company seemed perfect for me, since I love to cook for people and I would be able to do the work in the evenings and during weekends and holidays when I was not working as an HR manager during the week. I also knew that if I was going to start my own business, it would have to be something that I was passionate about since the business would take up what little bit of free time I had left.

For as long as I can remember, I wanted to be in the kitchen watching my grandmother stirring, whipping, rolling, and slicing all manner of ingredients into one delectable meal after another.

When I was old enough to actually assist in the cooking duties, I was immediately hooked. To me, those mouthwatering aromas that never failed to draw wide-eyed and smiling faces into the room seemed like the best way to express your love and appreciation to others. I became obsessed with honing the creativity, skill, and warmth one must possess to nurture something from a raw and unappetizing state into a meal capable of bringing so much joy and relief to people. HR work and cooking can be similar in that way, but cooking offers a more immediate vehicle to deliver those things than HR often can. Patience is still a requirement for both, however, but an undercooked chicken or cake has a way of teaching you the importance of that fact almost instantly.

After months of creating and perfecting my menu and marketing my new venture, I launched Windy Peach and couldn't believe how rapidly my client list grew. Before I knew it, I was getting spots on local and national television programs to promote the business, receiving invitations to appear with celebrity chefs, and regularly fielding requests to cater events for hundreds of guests. I greatly appreciated all of those opportunities and the quick success of the business, but I was still dedicated to my role as a manager of human resources for a large company. I realized that while I loved cooking, I didn't have enough passion for it to do it professionally long term. Less than a year after I launched Windy Peach, I was completely drained and decided to close down the business so I could focus more of my time and energy on my HR career.

I did not view my closing down Windy Peach as a failure. Not long after closing the business and focusing solely on my HR career, I was promoted to vice president of human resources and put in charge of my own department. I had proven to myself that I had the potential to run my own business and that it could be as successful as I wanted it to be. I'm grateful for that experience, mostly because it forced me to be honest with myself about what I really wanted to do while showing me the possibilities of what I could do. Windy Peach had encouraged my entrepreneurial aspirations; I just needed to find an outlet for it that was more fulfilling to me than catering.

That's to say that Windy Peach did not really *learn* me. I met my true self through leading my own HR department. Exploring different careers at a young age helped me to merge my passions and sense of personal potential with the right profession. It wasn't easy, but for me it was a necessary process to finding my calling, so to speak.

As a CEO, part of my job now is to help my employees understand how they can apply their passions to their job and discover their own potential. The importance of that type of work is increasingly common in thought leadership conversations today, which often stress that CEOs and managers should make concepts like employee engagement, human capital, retention, and potential a priority in their leadership training. Let's take a more detailed look at why those concepts have been receiving so much attention over the last decade and what they really mean.

EXPLORING DIFFERENT CAREERS AT A YOUNG AGE HELPED ME TO MERGE MY PASSIONS AND SENSE OF PERSONAL POTENTIAL WITH THE RIGHT PROFESSION.

THE TROUBLE WITH TALENT:
IDENTIFYING AND SUPPORTING POTENTIAL

Across size and industry, companies are searching for ways to stay compatible with progress in a wide range of areas, but few are as charged as the topic of talent management. With baby boomers and early Gen Xers moving into retirement while millennials and Gen Zers remain relatively difficult for traditional business models to engage, the race to perfect attracting and retaining high-potential talent has accelerated the search for solutions exponentially in recent years.

Why? Well, to be fair, it's not without its warranted reasons. Unfortunately, much of the discomfort and inefficiency workplaces are feeling today stems from management styles and mindsets that are no longer, or perhaps never really were, good for enhancing employee potential. The increasingly archaic frameworks of level after level of relative strangers exhausting themselves for a purpose they don't completely understand are beginning to grind themselves into extinction. What the progress we've seen so far has shown is that while corporations built these models from the best information available at the time—within the constraints, demands, and needs of their former environment, to be sure—they aren't enabling people to do their best work in today's environment, especially now that the COVID-19 pandemic has shaken up most work structures around the world.

You could make the argument that if employees work harder and longer, they'll be rewarded financially, but even monetary compensation has its limits. The rising popularity of such concepts as social responsibility and conscious capitalism over the last several years has made it clear that many people are seeking to identify purpose in nearly all aspects of their life. If high-potential talent is not being driven by something larger than a paycheck or receiving more accommodation for their actual needs and wants—whether it be more flexibility to help care for their families or stronger job assurance—employers will inevitably get a diminished level of productivity out of their people, or they'll lose them altogether. For employers waiting for the momentum of this particular workforce movement to blow over, if the pre-COVID theoretical fervor and now the pandemic-induced needs and practicalities sustain the way most experts predict they will, they may be left waiting in a talent vacuum for too long to see the swing return.

Workforce and workplace trends rarely, if ever, return once they change. Until the 1990s, the average professional found it reasonable to move from college graduation to a full-time job and build a career with just one or two companies until retirement.

Workers with a complete lack of impermanence in their work situation clearly lead a very different approach and mindset when it comes to work and career building, most often looking for more from their work to help guide them. Where one of the most popular premises for workers has been to survive the grueling pace and machinelike expectations long enough to cash in their retirement benefits, most people want to actually enjoy their job, find a personal purpose in it, and be allowed the freedom to do it better. In that way, the very concept of work as a struggle and a commonly thankless effort is receiving an inspiring rewrite.

But despite the opposing views of younger workers today as entitled and too idealistic, trending social awareness and sensitivity owes less to the fragility of one group compared to another than it does to the timing of social, economic, and now public health turbulence and its lingering impacts. Of course, these difficulties forced all workers to adapt and grow more resourceful to weather the storm, and many have emerged better prepared for the workplace as a result.

In a time when jobs require a growing number of skills to execute diversified and creative-based tasks while wages stay comparatively stagnate, a worker's loyalty to their company has come to be determined by whether their employers really care about the job they're doing. Purpose, merit, autonomy, and respect are now as primary in the minds of most workers as promotions, benefits packages, and bonuses, as many workers seem more content turning away from companies that fail to align with their core values. For leaders looking to nurture a more stable workforce, they're learning that they must prove to their workers that they and their work matter by supporting the ways in which they can do their best work. COVID-related concerns have also pushed many traditional workplaces to operate differently, such as working remotely, but if they're more committed to the company, engaged in their work, and producing better results, the flexibility is an easy trade to make.

A major reason behind companies with talent retention problems is a failure to establish and articulate a company purpose and culture that enables workers to connect to their work. It's a long and winding path to take, but for a talent management regiment to succeed in the expanding global marketplace, employing either a global workforce or a local workforce that can also work wherever they want, it will not get the talent it needs to be successful without first coming to thoroughly understand its talent pool.

The opportunity in front of business leaders now, as the designers of work and the workplace and of our roles therein, is to start connecting what we know to be true about people and their potential to innovative approaches to human capital. Maximizing the economic value of a workforce, whether through its collective knowledge and skill or otherwise, is all part of the same conversation, after all.

If people are companies' dearest assets, then they should be viewed as invaluable resources whose potential should be nurtured. Leaders need to understand how employees flourish as well as when they are at risk. Individuals also need to understand their potential and how to progress it into an actual, useable resource; otherwise both the employer and the employee suffer from the missed opportunities.

Many organizations have gotten that message and are now experimenting with alternatives to hierarchical models and flexible workplace arrangements—anything that may drive advantageous change in the workplace.

Other strategies have begun to unfurl from the same conceptual

IF PEOPLE ARE COMPANIES' DEAREST ASSETS, THEN THEY SHOULD BE VIEWED AS INVALUABLE RESOURCES WHOSE POTENTIAL SHOULD BE NURTURED.

mast, an emphasis on employee health and wellness chief among them. Emotional health, stemming from fulfillment, ease and comfort, and recognition, is now nearly as critical as health screenings or financial acumen training. We must openly address the cost of working in an environment every day where people are trying to do their best and bring their full self but are not able, or comfortable, to do so. Most of us will spend the majority of our adult lives working. If it's not a place where people's fullest potential can thrive, then we pay a grave price—and so does the business.

I was fortunate to find where my passion for helping people and a career could overlap as an HR specialist, which would not have been possible without a great mentor and the opportunity to lead my own department fairly early in my career. Before I started my own company, my former employers created a department for me to run. That vote of confidence was a boost to believing in myself and my potential to be a great leader. I was driven and ambitious, hungry to prove wrong those who had rejected or doubted me, but I still found myself feeling short on self-confidence.

Having a department created specifically for me and being allowed to run it however I saw fit allowed me to see a bigger and brighter future for myself than I had previously imagined. I soon found myself outgrowing my position, however, as I needed more control to institute my team's more ambitious and far-reaching ideas. I had also been promised stock options in the company as part of my pay package, a promise that still had not been fulfilled nearly a year after I accepted the position.

One afternoon, I returned to the office after leaving to retrieve something I had forgotten and unexpectedly walked into a senior executive meeting. As I opened the door, I heard the owner of the company remark to his team, "I'll never give that n****r part of my business." Stunned but not necessarily shocked by his overt racism, I turned and left the building. It took a long time for the sting to subside, but hearing his feelings about me in such a flagrant way lit a fire in me that I hadn't had in quite some time. With the confidence of having run my own department and launching a successful side business, that fire to prove this man wrong was the missing ingredient to my starting a human resources–focused company of my own. Now I just needed to take the leap of faith and put my growing self-confidence, determination, and potential to work for myself.

CHAPTER FOUR

FEAR

I was twenty-six when I started Elements, my current company. At the time, when I envisioned what a CEO looked like, I saw a straight, white, older man somewhere between fifty and seventy years old, an image starkly opposite from my own identity and experiences. CEOs were mostly depicted as such in movies, in magazines, and on television because most CEOs are, in fact, white men over the age of fifty.[1] That identity was my reference point for what a CEO should be, and it left me with a lot of insecurities and fears regarding my place as CEO—even if it was my own company. What would clients think? Would they be concerned about my age, worried that I didn't have the experience or know-how to solve their problems? Would they feel uncomfortable with my race or sexuality? I didn't know, but I knew that I didn't feel comfortable putting myself in the CEO

---

1   Chip Cutter, "CEOs Under 50 Are a Rare Find in the S&P 500," *Wall Street Journal*, May 22, 2019, https://www.wsj.com/articles/ ceos-under-50-are-a-rare-find-in-the-s-p-500-11558517401; Phil Wahba, "The Number of Black CEOs in the Fortune 500 Remains Very Low," *Fortune*, June 1, 2020, https://fortune.com/2020/06/01/ Black-ceos-fortune-500-2020-african-american-business-leaders/.

spotlight so soon into my first serious entrepreneurial endeavor.

I had a lot of experience with sales and felt comfortable as a salesperson, so I decided that I would tell everyone I was the VP of sales and present the CEO as a mysterious figure to every client. For two years, I ran the organization like a sales firm and pretended that I was not the CEO of my company. That worked out well at the time, as we were a young company and needed to continuously increase our sales numbers quickly to facilitate and sustain enough growth to survive our competition.

My fear of publicly "outing" myself as CEO had multiple origins. I was afraid that my identity as a young, Black, gay man might hamper my company's ability to land contracts and grow. I fretted over what the climate and repercussions, if any, might be like due to our being a Black-owned business in an international market. I was insecure about my lack of experience in a CEO role, fearing that I would not be taken seriously by current and prospective clients. Most of all, I feared failing.

I had some degree of fear that if I was the public face of the company and the company failed, then that failure would be mine and mine alone for everyone to see. After two years, however, we were thriving. I had done the hard part of founding and leading a company to early success, and that instilled in me the confidence to reveal to clients who I really was. I worked up the courage to tell every existing client that I was the CEO, and in comparatively undramatic fashion, the general response from clients and colleagues was, well, indifference. That didn't mean that my fears of failure vanished, of course, but it did relieve some of the pressure I was putting on myself.

Being honest about who I was and taking full ownership of my position gave me a renewed sense of self-confidence and purpose, as well as a stronger commitment to the company I was building and higher expectations for what we could accomplish. Fear wanted me to bury my head in sales charts—where I had felt most comfortable—rather than take on the broader duties of a CEO. Overcoming the fears of what people outside the company might think about me as a CEO as well as the fear of being "the boss" rather than a friend or colleague took courage, but it also showed me how useful fear can be in your life. Use it as a motivator and guide. Learn to embrace fear, and you will discover your own ways of controlling it, of pointing it in the direction you're trying to go and allowing it to serve

LEARN TO EMBRACE FEAR, AND YOU WILL DISCOVER YOUR OWN WAYS OF CONTROLLING IT, OF POINTING IT IN THE DIRECTION YOU'RE TRYING TO GO AND ALLOWING IT TO SERVE AS THE FUEL YOU NEED TO PROPEL YOU THROUGH THE ROUGH PATCHES.

as the fuel you need to propel you through the rough patches and many obstacles you're sure to encounter along whatever life and career paths you decide to take.

EVERY SECOND COUNTS:
TAKING SMALL STEPS AGAINST THE FEARS THAT ARE HOLDING US BACK

We have the same 86,400 seconds in each day as everyone else, yet some people manage to do more every day than others. Much of the reason for why that is has to do with fear. We tend to fear the unknown—the obstacles, pitfalls, and dead ends that, whether real or imagined, we believe will be lying in wait for us should we even try to pursue what we really want in life. It's the uncertainty of the future that holds so many people back, where they surrender their aspirations to the comforting familiarities of their present life. Sometimes we just need to see that it's possible first, that there is a way to achieve a dream or goal, and then, with enough courage, we can go make it happen for ourselves.

If you forget about how you think someone is going to respond and ask that question you've been wanting to ask them, or take that chance in your career that you've been putting off, or make the move you've been too scared to make, you will find great value in the results. Even if things don't turn out exactly how you may have wished they would, you will have proven to yourself that fear is not ruling your life. Accomplishments are not reached due to an absence of fear; they are reached in spite of it. They are reached by fostering what begins as a small kernel of courage over time, until whatever fears you may have feel smaller, more manageable, and are no longer providing the defining limits you put upon yourself or your business. If you can give yourself just ten seconds of all your courage to take the first step toward overcoming a fear, you'll at least allow enough time for the universe to show up on your side.

Sometimes it's in those ten seconds of tremendous courage that the greatest things happen. It's the opportunities that I let fear alone talk me out of that I end up regretting the most. What's worse, I've found, is that when I give in to a particular fear, I'm actually helping to strengthen all my other fears as well. By surrendering to a fear, we inadvertently feed the self-doubt, anxiety, insecurity, and pessimism that exist within all of us. That leads us to even more fear and an increased susceptibility of caving to it. Refuse to take any action against fear for long enough, and you may find it controlling every aspect of your life.

The parts of ourselves that we let fear rule over manifest themselves in the things we continue to procrastinate on, neglect, or try to avoid entirely. I'm still guilty of letting fear win. I still have moments every day in which I'm not as confident and courageous as I want to be. I'm not perfect, but I can't think of any meaningful thing I've ever done that didn't begin with a profound sense of vulnerability and fear. I also can't think of a time when I stood in that vortex of vulnerability and fear and kept pushing forward that didn't lead to someone stepping up and saying, "Thank you. That's inspiring. I've been there too. How can I help?" or "Thank you. That's comforting. I'm there now. I need help." There's a time and a place for everything, but generally

RAISING ENOUGH COURAGE TO TAKE THE FIRST STEP TOWARD WHAT YOU REALLY WANT IS ALL IT TAKES TO DISCOVER THAT FEAR IS LYING TO YOU.

speaking, raising enough courage to take the first step toward what you really want is all it takes to discover that fear is lying to you.

The battle between fear and courage is not a strictly personal one either. Fear of the unknown is one reason why representation is so important, both in and out of the workplace. Many large organizations suffer from a leaky workforce pipeline, which often stems from a lack of representation. If people do not see themselves represented in the senior leadership team, if they see themselves repeatedly passed over for opportunities, if they perceive that they have to work twice as hard to keep pace, they will eventually either disengage from their work or take their skills elsewhere. It is critical to construct a system that guides and cultivates talent from the entry level to the top, creating channels of communication through which every group has a voice and everyone benefits by listening. This is the beginning of forging the path to workplace equity, one in which fear is not allowed to restrict an individual's capabilities and restrain an organization's potential.

A larger but connected trend is the democratization of decision-making as a society. We see this in the way people research their purchasing decisions; crowdsource funding to bring an idea to fruition or meet a need; evaluate an employer before interviewing or taking a job; and leverage social media. Though far from level, one's mobility and potential are increasingly less hindered by identity markers like class, race, gender, sexuality, nationality, etc. today than they were in past decades. Technology is the most notable driver behind this change, providing the individual with an unprecedented level of access to knowledge, training, employment opportunities, self-empowerment, and authority. To varying degrees, work cultures in the United States and beyond have moved away from rigid, military-like hierarchies in order to accommodate the agility, adaptiveness, specialization, and inclusiveness that so many modern industries require.

Like most changes in society, this democratic shift has its roots in the disenchantment of the youth. It's not exactly rare for people to lose at least some faith in their institutions and begin to view authority with a critical eye, whether that occurs as they breach the threshold of adulthood or after they are well past it. For generations raised during America's manufacturing prime, many watched their expectations of long-term employment stability virtually vanish during their lifetime. For the millennial generation they raised, the trend toward autonomy, self-reliance, and adaptability grew, but so, too, did the importance of purpose and meaning in relation to one's work and life.

Being embraced for who they are might have begun with the stereotypical, overly doting parenting styles with which some were raised, but it stems from the hardships that many older workers experienced and the hope that their children or grandchildren will not have to endure them as well. And while the stereotype of younger generations demanding purpose, fulfillment, and a paycheck from their job might be criticized as entitlement or laziness, in my opinion a fairer statement to employers begins to surface from this generation: "If you value me, invest in me and see all of me so I can do my best work for you."

Stereotypes are almost always motivated by fear. Whether a perceived threat is physical, economic, or purely psychological in nature, fear will try its best to decide our response. Because fear blurs the line between reality and delusion, we often rely on stereotypes to cope with or run away from our fears rather than face them directly. A person or company that has not confronted their fears head-on is allowing those same fears to inform their decisions, which show up in everything from the speed and scale of personal or company growth to how they manage competition to the way they represent themselves and/or their company. Without fair representation, it's hard to push through the fears, disillusionment, or skepticisms that may be keeping a person from pursuing their greatest ambitions.

A PERSON OR COMPANY THAT HAS NOT CONFRONTED THEIR FEARS HEAD-ON IS ALLOWING THOSE SAME FEARS TO INFORM THEIR DECISIONS.

Whether you or someone else feels like they aren't fairly represented in an organization—which leads to fear that one will not receive fair treatment or that success in general may be more difficult or even impossible—or if you find yourself feeling paralyzed by your own fears to make a leap of faith on yourself, your business, or something else, you can begin to chip away at that fear with daily acts that require your courage. I'm not talking about running into a burning building, going bungee jumping, or spontaneously quitting your job tomorrow.

I'm talking about small acts of courage that are relative to where you are in your relationship with fear.

An act of courage may be as small as forcing yourself to finish that project you've been procrastinating over due to fears that it will not meet your or someone else's expectations, or as large as telling someone you care about a painful truth, committing yourself to starting your own company, or even leaving the company you have built. Courage is built over time, a process that's easiest when you face your fears in incremental order, from small to large. The degree of fear you feel toward something is generally proportional to how confident you feel in your ability to face and defeat fear in general.

Ten seconds of the kind of courage that surprises you is all it takes to beat back fear just long enough for more realistic possibilities to come into view. Ask yourself: "What do I want for my life? Where am I, and where do I want to go? What kind of person am I, and what kind of person do I want to be?" Then identify what your first step needs to be to get there, nurture courage over fear, and take it.

CHAPTER FIVE

COURAGE

Though I would have never admitted it at the time, I was terrified when I quit my position as VP of HR to found my own company. I knew how to run a department within a company, and I'd had several years' worth of experience managing other people, but I knew very little about owning and operating a company, especially one with employees and clients scattered throughout the world.

Everyone's preference that I stay with a stable, well-paying salary job weighed into my decision as well, especially my grandmother's. Although she passed away before I formally launched Elements Global Services, I had shared with her contemplations of starting my own company. We both knew that I would not have a steady income for years, if ever, should I quit my job in order to build and run my own business, but I worried less over the chances of my success than my grandmother did. In her view, I had "made it." I had a high-power position in a secure career field making six figures plus benefits, and I'd gotten it all before the age of thirty. Why I would be willing to give all of that up so I could take on more stress and work longer hours for less pay completely eluded her, and sometimes me, and for good reason.

Age and generational elements obviously played starring roles in my grandmother's concerns, presumably seeing my willingness to take on the risks of entrepreneurship as naive, overconfident, or simply irresponsible—all of which would have been correct observations at the time. After all, my experience as a firstborn male raised in upper-middle-class, suburban Chicago in the 1990s was quite different from her experience as a Black woman growing up in rural Jim Crow–era Georgia a half century earlier. Her opportunities and choices were greatly limited from the time she was born, her life's potential largely predetermined by strangers on the basis of race and gender. Even though her father owned a general store and a funeral home, she saw firsthand the hardships that came with success in the midcentury South. She and her family became targets of the Ku Klux Klan and others due to their successes in business and education. I have my own set of obstacles of course, but I also had the benefit of living in a time and place in which the individual has greater entrepreneurial opportunities thanks to technological advancements, social progress, and a generational culture that encourages autonomy and risk-taking over a steady paycheck, especially if in pursuit of self-actualization (i.e., fulfilling an individual's potential).

Despite my inexperience working in a CEO capacity, my grandmother's concerns for my general well-being, and my fears of being a failure, I remained determined to challenge myself. If there were to be limits on what I could achieve, I reasoned, then I wanted to be the one deciding what and where they would be. Ultimately, my decision to take on the risks involved centered on two personal truths: one, everyone deserves to be treated with respect and fairness; and two, I get to decide the limits of my potential, not anyone else. It was the unfulfilled promises from my former employer that made it clear to me that I had to move on.

The best way I could ensure that I worked for a company that allowed those principles to manifest fully would be to start my own.

As I said in the last chapter, courage is not fearlessness. It's the act of denying fear's power to stop you from pursuing something you want or need. Courage is not recklessness either. It's smarter than that. Regardless of one's level of courage and confidence, risks must still be thoroughly and rationally assessed. Risk-taking without careful deliberation and preparation is based more on carelessness and arrogance than courage. In other words, you must have at least a basic understanding of the risks and consequences involved for courage to exist.

YOU MUST HAVE AT LEAST A BASIC UNDERSTANDING OF THE RISKS AND CONSEQUENCES INVOLVED FOR COURAGE TO EXIST.

Behind the deployment of that courage is the notion that the potential for a positive outcome is greater than the potential for a negative outcome. Much, if not all, of the ways we make those discernments hail from our attitude, perspective, and the relationship we have with fear and reality. In that way, if you want courage to play a larger role in your decision-making process as a CEO, entrepreneur, or leader in general, you first need to learn as much as you can about the risks, consequences, and perceptions that come with being a leader. Let's look at some of them now.

RARE, REVERED, AND REVILED:
MANAGING THE PERCEPTIONS AND REALITIES OF LEADERSHIP

When you start a business for the first time, you will receive a number of shocks and disappointments. The costs *will* shock you, and some of the people you thought you could trust *will* disappoint you. The number of legal hoops to navigate and amount of "paperwork" to manage will exhaust you, and the grueling hours spent working on the so-called frontlines will merge with even more hours fretting over decisions that will either make or break you as well as anyone else depending on you to make good choices. Unfortunately, this is an unavoidable reality.

I only tell you this to reiterate that starting a business and/or leading one is hard, and sometimes it will be even harder than you had imagined it would, or could, be. But it's also extremely fulfilling. We tend to think of a business owner or leader as someone who makes the most money, comes and goes as they please, and gets to call all the shots. They're the boss, the kingpin, the person everyone wants to please, right? With that image in mind, you may be asking, "How bad could it really be?"

The myth that the owner has it better than everyone else is usually the first misconception to crumble once you actually become one. It's a necessary humbling for anyone who became an entrepreneur for the wrong reasons, however, but it will get easier as you adjust to the new role and the life that comes with it.

People don't often realize how small the reward can be being a business owner in the beginning. Whatever glamour you may be fortunate enough to find in the beginning (e.g., status, popularity, money, promotional giveaways, schedule flexibility) is usually outweighed by the amount of pressure and responsibilities you're still adjusting to carrying on your shoulders. If you don't feel that weight, then you probably aren't committing yourself fully to the business and the people in it. So let me dispel any delusions of grandeur you may have now: as an entrepreneur, you are the last person to be paid and the first person responsible for missteps, no matter where they occur or who commits them.

Before you see a penny, you will have to put your savings on the line, or someone else's if you are able to convince an investor to take a chance on you. That means you will be putting your, your family's, and/or someone else's well-being in jeopardy as well. You will put all of your relationships in jeopardy, too, due to the amount of work and time that starting a business typically requires. I lost three relationships to my business, largely because I couldn't make enough time for my partners.

AS AN ENTREPRENEUR, YOU ARE THE LAST PERSON TO BE PAID AND THE FIRST PERSON RESPONSIBLE FOR MISSTEPS, NO MATTER WHERE THEY OCCUR OR WHO COMMITS THEM.

When a business first opens, not only will you most likely fall into debt and lose friends, but you'll probably be among the lowest-paid people in your business—if you can afford to pay yourself at all. You will be the first person in and the last person out every day, and you will still have to deal with the mental stress of planning for tomorrow. You have the ultimate amount of pressure, and you're doing all of this while most of the rewards are reaped by your staff and customers. It stays this way for the majority of business owners until either their loans are repaid or the business is financially secure enough to extract a decent income for yourself. During that process, everybody else wins. It is a relatively thankless yet vital position that may or may not pay off in the long run. With so much on the line, the uncertainty is terrifying, and if you're not expecting it, the lack of acknowledgment can be as deafening as it is discouraging.

Once you see all of this in motion, a few things become clear about the important role an entrepreneur plays within a society that inspire a greater sense of purpose in your work. You realize that for every dollar you sell in your business, not only are you helping to support yourself and your employees, but you're also supporting utility companies, suppliers, technicians, tradespeople, lawyers, accountants, state, local, and federal tax systems, and more. As an entrepreneur, you're moving more money through the economy than are most people. Understanding exactly how you contribute to the economic ecosystem is an uplifting element of the entrepreneurial experience, one that will serve you well if and when you begin to doubt yourself and your efforts.

When you are a business owner, you will see how many people are benefiting from what you have started, and that's a truly moving and satisfying realization to experience. Getting connected to all the moving parts of your business helps remove the villainy of being "the boss" that you may struggle with in the beginning, or even long afterward when the business is scaling.

SOME HARD TRUTHS ABOUT ENTREPRENEURSHIP

It's important to distinguish yourself between a CEO and an entrepreneur early. In the public sphere, there are really two definitions of the word *CEO*: one applies to an entrepreneur who built their own company from the ground up, and the other applies to an outside, hired employee. I think a true entrepreneur is a **chief innovation officer**. They're constantly coming up with a new idea or a new direction. They're the visionary of the organization, an innovator who creates something out of nothing.

A CEO who's hired by an existing organization is usually more of a **chief efficiency officer**. Their job is to come into an organization and make it more efficient. They're typically the leader of an organization that has already been envisioned and built but needs to be improved and strengthened in key areas like production and operation costs, employee recruitment and retention, public relations, market expansion, and overall profitability in general.

The image of the latter type of CEO who's running a multibillion-dollar company and making millions every year usually gets a bad rap among the general public. The average CEO makes around $14 million a year, according to a 2018 report from research and consultancy firm Pearl Meyer and Partners.[2] The salary sounds outrageous, sure, and maybe it is. Even if you recognize the impact the CEO has on the economic ecosystem, including how many people's jobs thrive based on the decisions that one person makes, it's hard to justify why someone should make $14 million a year to help run someone else's company. But consider this: If that CEO grows the business they manage by even 5 percent, then they have helped their company inject many times more than $14 million into the economy. That growth will create more jobs in their own organization as well as in the other industries that their company's money touches. The media rarely popularizes that aspect, and as a result, people tend to develop a cynical view of CEOs. And while there are surely some bad people out there who serve as CEOs, the position itself plays an important role in sustaining a healthy economy.

Because the role of a CEO is often vilified, however, the entrepreneur's job is that much more difficult. You must face the poor image the title conjures among much of the public, which in turn will likely exist among your employees too. Unless you are able to tune out the negativity and focus on how you contribute to society in a positive way, regardless of whether or not you're ever recognized for it, the job will be grueling and maybe even feel pointless. Humility, clarity

---

2   Deb Lifshey, "The CEO Pay Ratio: Data and Perspectives from the 2018 Proxy Season," Harvard Law School Forum on Corporate Governance, October 14, 2018, https://corpgov.law.harvard.edu/2018/10/14/the-ceo-pay-ratio-data-and-perspectives-from-the-2018-proxy-season/.

around your purpose, self-confidence, and the courage to manage that stigma anyway will serve you well here.

Another factor in the perception of CEOs and entrepreneurs has to do with their impact on wageworkers, which comprises a large percentage of the media coverage relating to CEOs and entrepreneurs. "Are they hurting more than helping the economy and the society that depends upon it?" That's the general storyline we see and read about most often, so it's important to understand that dynamic as well.

All positions and wages are based, to some degree, on skill and comparable capability to hire that position. If there's no one willing to work for less than you, your wage is likely to remain flat. On the other hand, if there are capable people willing to work for less than you, your wage is going to drop. This is the grim side to supply and demand. Most of us might love it when companies like Amazon provide such an expansive marketplace (supply) that the price for almost everything they sell drops due to increased transparency and competition, but we hate it when that same law of economics affects our paycheck. After all, we're not talking about products and services but rather people and their livelihoods. Consequently, every entrepreneur will have to negotiate this challenge at some point in time.

Regardless of the bigger picture, some degree of villainy is going to come with being a business owner or leader no matter what you do. There will also be certain "necessary evils" to your position. As a business owner, be prepared to negotiate your business decisions against people's perceptions of them. It's a very fine line to walk, as you must assess carefully how you sustain your business without alienating your customer base or losing your employees' faith and trust in you to be both a smart businessperson and a good leader who is strong, compassionate, and fair. So much of that has to do with your ability not only to continually improve the value of your company but your skills as a manager and leader as well.

IT'S LONELY AT THE TOP

If you are like me, you enjoy rooting for the underdog. It's inspiring to see someone deserving win against all odds, whether in business, sports, entertainment, academics, or something else. As soon as they're victorious, though, many of us are tempted to want to see them lose. Why is it not inspiring to see someone win and continue to win? Winning one game isn't nearly as difficult as winning a hundred, after all, so why do most people dislike a person, company, or program that regularly outperforms their competitors?

I believe the answer lies in our tendency to attribute dominance to unfairness. "You caught an easy break," some might say. "Oh, you screwed someone; you had to have," say others. Luck and cheating are popular rationalizations for a person's, or a company's, long-term successes, for reasons as varied and complicated as the individuals who make them. That cognitive dissonance can be easier to handle if we aren't in control. It's easier to change our minds than it is to change our actions, and it's more comforting to say that someone got lucky or did something wrong than it is to believe that someone accepted the risks, worked hard, persevered over myriad failures and challenges, and made sacrifices to get into their position. That's okay. You have to accept that there will be people who are going to criticize any success you have, no matter what you do or how you do it.

If your business is successful for a number of years, you should see an upgrade in your financial position as well. Money is one of those strange things that everyone needs and wants, but the people who go out and get it are generally loathed by those who do not. Some of that sentiment is legitimate, of course. There are plenty of people who inherit massive amounts of wealth and wield it in damaging ways, or who commit unethical and/or illegal acts to obtain their wealth. But I would argue that the majority of wealthy people obtain their wealth through hard work and self-discipline.

As a business owner, one of the things that is inevitable, no matter how much you try, is a gradual thinning of the herd with regard to your personal relationships. The prevailing nature of running a business is to have very little free time, which certainly puts a heavy strain on your personal relationships. If your business is successful, then finances and the lifestyle changes that often come with them can widen the gap even further between you and your friends. Over time, you may be able to afford to do things you've always wanted to do, such as taking vacations to far-off destinations, dining at high-end restaurants, or moving to a different neighborhood or city. Because most of our friendships are based on things that we relate to, your social circle may narrow despite your best intentions and efforts.

You may be able to pay yourself a robust salary as the company's profits rise, but beware that more money in your pocket comes with its own set of challenges too. You may begin to worry about people's intentions, for example, questioning whether they genuinely like or care about you or secretly want to use you for their own gain. As an entrepreneur, your position—both in terms of financial priorities and free time—is unrelatable to most people as well. Your interests, problems, and lifestyle as an entrepreneur are often considerably different when compared to the average person. That decrease in shared day-to-day experiences and relatable points of view coupled with disparities in available time and finances can, and likely will, put a strain on even your closest relationships.

The severity of that strain is usually proportional to each party's commitment to the relationship in question but also one's limitations in available time and energy to distribute to their personal relationships. Your entrepreneurial pursuits may force you into prioritizing the relationships you want to maintain the most while having to accept the loss of others.

There is a bright side to your life as an entrepreneur, of course. The autonomy of being your own employer is incredibly liberating, especially for those with an entrepreneurial spirit who typically find working for someone else too constraining. You also make broad and deep connections with others through your service. The relative freedom to steer the purpose of your work and life and the loosened restrictions on your income potential and general quality of life are just a few of the perks. As you grow as an entrepreneur, your interests and assets will expand, and so, too, will your social circles. You will find many more people who think like you, dream like you, and appreciate the vision you have of the world and your place in it.

It takes courage to leap into entrepreneurship, but when you do, you will find a community of people with whom you have an immediate connection due to the commonalities of your relatively rare set of personal characteristics and professional realities. It's exhilarating to live your life to the fullest. And even if the ride ends up having fewer passengers than you might have liked or expected, those who come along with you are special. The bonds you build with them will be some of the most genuine and meaningful relationships you will ever have.

At the same time, you cannot allow the "perks" of being an entrepreneur or CEO from blinding you to the realities of your duties. Ultimately, an entrepreneur and/or CEO is responsible for protecting and uplifting their company and, to a certain degree, everyone connected to it. In that effort, your connection to the experiences of everyone involved in the company is an unparalleled priority. Your ability to understand the needs and efforts of your workforce will shape how well you recruit and retain the people who ultimately execute your ideas and goals. In essence, these people decide whether the company's dreams come true or not. The challenge of recruitment, retention, and the sustainability of your dream lies in the people you choose to be a part of that dream.

CHAPTER SIX

RESPECT

Common courtesy, manners, the way we greet people with a "hello" or a smile, how we express our appreciation or gratefulness with a "thank you"—all of these things may fall into the category of respect, but respect goes deeper than that. Accepted or preferred social graces are an indication that someone has respect for you or is at least making an effort to be respectful of you. Even a surface-level display of respect is, generally speaking, intended to be the first step toward a good relationship, regardless of how long or brief that relationship may be. Whether it's an important business or personal relationship or your server at a restaurant, if you struggle with giving respect to others, then it's going to be difficult for you to create a mutually enjoyable experience with anyone. It's going to be even harder to lead others in a manner that empowers them to perform at their best.

Respect in the context of business leadership refers to the mutual appreciation for one another. Regular acts of disregard for the well-being of others obviously do not foster respect or civility, but they also hinder the ability of two people or groups of people to be productive, effective, or innovative—key elements of success in business. Being disrespectful only breeds contempt for one another, making compromise and efficient progress toward dually beneficial goals more unlikely. That's why I believe that being respectful of others is a critical first step toward building trust and collaboration with them. Perhaps more importantly, showing basic respect and decency to someone you may disagree with is the best way to exchange ideas in a more receptive environment, which begets more productivity and increases everyone's chances of gaining better outcomes than the alternative.

The ability to extend respect to others depends on how well we negotiate disagreement. That's why it's critical to be *reflective* as opposed to *reactive* when navigating differences, which you will have to do regularly as a business leader. You can use a three-step process to negotiate conflict: *experience, response, outcome* (a.k.a. E + R = O). Give a response to an experience in order to produce an outcome you expect or want. The R can be reactive or reflective. Reactive is emotional and impulsive. Reflective uses wisdom and skills learned from experience to resolve a problem with respect and tact. You can either "win" the interaction, or you can create a positive outcome for all.

To some, it may seem as though respect is a commonsense approach to leadership. In fairness, that is true, but it's also fair to acknowledge that many of us, leaders or not, are unsure how to communicate respect in a way that feels genuine to the intended party. Popular traditional philosophies around business leadership have advocated that leading a company should be based on establishing authority over direct reports. That strategy, however, allows room to neglect the importance of respect for others. Establishing authority should not come at the expense of treating people with respect. If a leader or manager scolded staff for any infraction, you may argue that they are just doing their job. But could they generate more effective results if they were simply more respectful in their reproach? I would argue that they could.

Consistent displays of disrespect usually sprout from a belief that others are not equal on some level. Respect for others is tantamount to building trust and forging authentic rela- tionships, but you cannot achieve that end without first knowing where respect for others is rooted. The answer is internal: you must respect yourself to respect others. Why? Because until you respect yourself,

YOU MUST RESPECT YOURSELF TO RESPECT OTHERS.

it's hard to believe in yourself. That may sound sappy or unrealistic, but consider this: If you truly believed in the values and character you strive to embody as a leader, you would not allow yourself to be disrespectful to others. In that way, respecting yourself and the person you aim to be requires you to be respectful of those around you.

Part of having respect for yourself is stepping away from bad influencers in your life. It is certainly easier to avoid people and situ- ations that make you feel uncomfortable, but isolationist mindsets that only preach to the choir rather than making a larger impact are extremely limiting to the quality of leadership you want to attain. Showing respect to those with different ideologies is essential to problem-solving. You cannot make good leadership decisions without hearing from as many angles as possible around a particular issue. That requires a culture that enables differing points of view and supports an open and respectful environment.

You can preach to the choir, or you can preach to the congre- gation. That decision is yours, but respect helps you reach a larger audience, build stronger relationships, garner more information and understanding, and ultimately make a greater impact with your life and work. Respect is the bridge to understanding, which ultimately builds better solutions and outcomes.

Politeness is sometimes mistaken for respect, and while they are similar, they are not the same. Politeness is the consideration of how you make someone else feel. Respect, on the other hand, is the action of showing someone else that you view them as an equal. For instance, a person may be polite to the grocery store clerk, restaurant worker, or delivery person, but do they really respect what they do? The global pandemic has altered that perception for many people, bringing genuine respect and appreciation for that work as opposed to casual politeness to the people who perform it. Respect is the manifestation of recognizing the genuine value of another person. That distinction is inherently contingent upon whether you actually respect who you are and/or the person you wish to become, and you cannot be an authentic leader until you do.

RECRUIT, RETAIN, AND REENERGIZE:
BENEFITS OF RESPECT IN THE WORKPLACE

Across size and industry, companies are searching for ways to stay compatible with progress in a wide range of areas, but few are as charged as the topic of talent management. With baby boomers and early Gen X workers beginning to move into retirement while the millennial and up-and-coming Gen Z generations remain relatively difficult for traditionalists to engage, the race to perfect attracting and retaining high-value talent has accelerated the search for solutions in recent years.

"Employee engagement" is a popular fixture in that search, due to its ties to employee recruitment, retention, productivity, and quality. The passion an employee feels for their job, their commitment to the company, and the degree of effort one puts into their work are the primary factors used to determine an employee's overall "engagement" in their job and/or the company that employs them. While some of their metrics can and often do overlap, employee satisfaction is not the same as employee engagement. Employee satisfaction, as its name suggests, only determines if a person is satisfied with their job or company, usually regarding compensation-to-effort ratios. Employee engagement, on the other hand, assesses an employee's level of motivation, involvement, and emotional commitment to a particular job or organization. In other words, employee satisfaction generally focuses on the level of contentment within a specific position or company, while employee engagement examines the fundamental drivers of performance among the company's workforce.

For most organizations, employee engagement as a motor for change is not an entirely altruistic shift. A 2017 study of 1,500 respondents by the Engagement Institute—a collaborative research, training, and consulting firm comprised of the Conference Board, Sirota-Mercer, Deloitte, ROI, the Culture Works, and Consulting LLP—reported that disengaged employees cost companies between $450 and $550 billion every year.[3] Meanwhile, a 2017 study from Gallup concluded that "the behaviors of highly engaged business units result in 21 percent greater profitability."[4] Additionally, a 2013 study by Harvard Business Review Analytic Services (an independent commercial research unit within the *Harvard Business Review*) found that 71 percent of the 500 business executives surveyed ranked employee engagement as "very important to achieving overall business success."[5]

---

3   Valerie Bolden-Barrett, "Study: Disengaged Employees Can Cost Companies Up to $550B a year," HRDrive.com, March 8, 2017, https://www.hrdive.com/news/study-disengaged-employees-can-cost-companies-up-to-550b-a-year/437606/.

4   Jim Harter and Annamarie Mann, "The Right Culture: Not Just about Employee Satisfaction," Gallup, April 12, 2017, https://www.gallup.com/workplace/236366/right-culture-not-employee-satisfaction.aspx.

5   *Harvard Business Review*, "The Impact of Employee Engagement on Performance," September 2013, https://hbr.org/resources/pdfs/comm/achievers/hbr_achievers_report_sep13.pdf.

Based on those numbers alone, it's not hard to see why disengagement in the workplace has become a core driver for leadership buy-in and motivation in recent years. We continue to seek out answers for why roughly 65 percent of workers are either actively disengaged or not engaged at work and, more importantly, how we can reverse the trend.[6]

According to a recent Gallup poll, employee engagement increased from 36 percent in 2020 to 39 percent by January of 2021—perhaps not surprisingly so, considering the many upheavals that 2020 brought along with it.[7] With an increasingly younger and more remote workforce ahead, employee engagement statistics help serve as a bellwether for the hurdles that lie ahead for employers if the needs of the modern worker aren't realized.

While the estimated $450 billion–plus in lost productivity of a largely nonengaged or actively disengaged workforce is nothing to shrug our shoulders at, pondering the impact that a largely uninterested workforce has on their company's efficiency and decision-making capabilities is even more disturbing. These may not be bad decisions per se, but they're likely to be the decisions tossed from the "yeah, whatever" mindset. It's not a stretch to assume that a "yeah, whatever" company won't be inspiring people to make great products or develop an excellent service any time soon, and the age of widespread social media and billion-dollar start-ups born from garages, dorm rooms, or virtually anywhere in the world is no time to be average.

The progress we've seen from the generational, social, technological, and economic movements over the last decade alone has shown that traditional large-scale management models aren't optimal at enabling people to do their best work in today's environment. As

6   Jim Harter, "U.S. Employee Engagement Rises following Wild 2020," Gallup, February 26, 2021, https://www.gallup.com/workplace/330017/employee-engagement-rises-following-wild-2020.aspx.

7   Jim Harter, "U.S. Employee Engagement Rises following Wild 2020."

more sectors and companies begin to interact with global markets and cultures, it's more common than ever for granular-level positions to be geographically dispersed and individually independent. COVID-19 pushed that trend into overdrive, and for many companies and positions, the temporary work-from-home solutions they found during the pandemic may become a permanent one.

A major reason behind companies with talent retention problems is a failure to establish and articulate a company purpose and culture that enables workers to connect with their work in a meaningful way and feel respected at the same time. It's a long and winding path to take, but for a talent management regiment to succeed in the expanding global marketplace, employing either a global workforce or a local workforce that can also work wherever they want, it will not get the talent it needs to be successful without first understanding its talent pool.

You could make the argument that if employees work harder and longer, they'll be rewarded financially. But even monetary compensation has its limits. Job burnout is far from a new phenomenon, but its importance in management strategies has grown in recent years as technological innovations have connected us to one another—and thus, for many, to our work—much more intimately. In 1978, the US Department of Justice published a report on job burnout as it related to "helping professionals," which were classified as those whose jobs "involve continuous, direct contact with different kinds of recipients (welfare clients, patients, prisoners, children)."[8]

The study's abstract asserts: "Over an extended period, emotional exhaustion can result from the stress of interpersonal contact. Many professionals experience a gradual loss of positive feelings, sympathy, and respect for their clients or patients. Often this leads to a cynical

---

8   C. Maslach, "Job Burnout—How People Cope," *Public Welfare* 36, no. 2 (Spring 1978): 56-58, https://www.ojp.gov/ncjrs/virtual-library/abstracts/job-burnout-how-people-cope.

and dehumanizing perception of clients that labels them in derogatory ways. Reports of burnout are highly correlated with workers' low morale, absenteeism, and high job turnover. Some people quit, change jobs, or leave the profession entirely." Even without the technology we have today enabling a seemingly limitless degree of interpersonal contact, workers and their leaders were struggling to deal with burnout from their jobs. What's more is that the concern was not only on the well-being of those dealing with "emotional exhaustion" but also the understanding that this kind of exhaustion could lead to poor job performance and negative impacts on client relations.

The abstract continues:

> People undergoing burnout often increase their use of alcohol and other drugs as a way of reducing tension and blotting out strong feelings of hostility and depression. They report more mental problems and often seek counseling over what they perceive to be their personal failing. People experiencing burnout often become involved in increased marital and family conflict as well. Professionals cope with burnout on an individual basis in various ways, such as psychologically withdrawing from difficult situations by intellectualizing, speaking to clients in superficial generalities, taking short breaks when a critical moment arises, and applying a formula rather than developing a unique solution to any given case. Other professionals deliberately engage in special activities that allow them to relax, such as physical exercise, meditating, etc.

The study concludes that "the development of training programs in interpersonal skills would help to better prepare professionals to work with their clients."

A 2015 study conducted by Deloitte on job burnout surveyed one thousand full-time, US-based professionals, reporting that 77 percent of respondents have experienced burnout at their current job and 42 percent have left a job specifically because they felt burned out. Those figures were higher when controlled for generation, with 84 percent of millennials saying they had experienced burnout at their current job and nearly 50 percent saying they had left a job because of it.[9]

The level of job burnout coupled with the rising popularity of such concepts as social responsibility and conscious capitalism over the last several years has made it clear that many people are seeking to identify purpose in nearly all aspects of their life. If high-potential talent is not being driven by something larger than a paycheck or receiving more accommodation for their actual needs and wants—whether it be more flexibility to help care for their families or stronger mobility opportunities—employers will inevitably get a diminished level of contribution from their best people or just lose them altogether. For employers waiting for the momentum of this particular workforce movement to blow over, if the present fervor sustains the way many researchers

> **IF HIGH-POTENTIAL TALENT IS NOT BEING DRIVEN BY SOMETHING LARGER THAN A PAYCHECK OR RECEIVING MORE ACCOMMODATION FOR THEIR ACTUAL NEEDS AND WANTS— WHETHER IT BE MORE FLEXIBILITY TO HELP CARE FOR THEIR FAMILIES OR STRONGER MOBILITY OPPORTUNITIES— EMPLOYERS WILL INEVITABLY GET A DIMINISHED LEVEL OF CONTRIBUTION FROM THEIR BEST PEOPLE OR JUST LOSE THEM ALTOGETHER.**

---

9   "Workplace Burnout Survey," Deloitte, accessed May 2021, https://www2. deloitte.com/us/en/pages/about-deloitte/articles/burnout-survey.html.

predict that it will, they may be left waiting in a talent vacuum for too long to see the swing return.

Workforce and workplace trends rarely, if ever, return once they change. In decades past, a comparatively smaller pool of degree holders and large employers enabled an individual to move more smoothly from college graduation to a company where they could spend their career until retirement, at least in theory. Today, however, companies are becoming smaller and more specialized than previous eras, employing fewer full-time employees in favor of gig workers to navigate the often-tenuous profit margins of markets and industries that are increasingly global.

We see companies grow and shrink incredibly quickly in this environment, making the financial and legal agility that contract workers provide even more alluring. The ability to bring in a team of specialized workers on a temporary basis when the tide is high and let them go if and when your fortunes change is extremely useful to a company, especially young ones. That kind of workforce agility does not come without a cost, though. Respect must still be shown and rewarded, of course, but understand that the ways in which respect shows up in today's workplace may look a little different than it did before the exponential advancements made in personal technology, the collision of America's two largest generations in the workforce, and a global pandemic changed so much about the way we live, work, and interact.

Workers with little to no sense of permanence in their job must have a mindset of self-reliance in their approach to career building, most often relying more on their individual work to guide them and open doors for them more than a single employer over a long period of time. Where the common premise for workers was once to survive at one company long enough to cash in their retirement benefits, the trend now is that workers want to actually like their job, find a personal purpose in it, and be given the freedom to do it better. In that way, the notion of work as a necessary but begrudging ritual of suffering has been receiving an inspiring rewrite.

Despite criticisms of younger workers today as being entitled, lazy, and too idealistic, trending social awareness and sensitivity owes less to the fragility of one group compared with another than it does to the timing of social and economic turbulence and its lingering impacts. Of course, the difficulties experienced over the last ten-plus years (e.g., wars, two recessions, worldwide civil and political unrest, and a deadly pandemic) have forced virtually all workers to adapt and grow more resourceful to weather the storms, and many have emerged better prepared for the modern work world as a result.

In a time when many jobs require a wider range of skills and knowledge to execute diversified and/or creative-based tasks for companies experiencing regular fluctuation, a worker's loyalty to their company is increasingly influenced by whether they feel their employer respects them and the work they do for the company. Purpose, merit, autonomy, and respect are now replacing the promotions race, benefits packages, and even plump bonuses, as workers seem more willing to turn away from companies that fail to align with them on a personal level. For companies to nurture a healthier, more stable workforce, they're learning that they must prove to their workers that they and their work matter by supporting the ways in which they can do their best work. In traditional workplaces, that may result in people working a little differently than they once did—such as working remotely, greater schedule flexibility, opportunities for volunteering or civic engagement, and/or better physical and mental health support. But if they're more committed to the company, engaged in their work, and producing better results, certain accommodations should be an easy trade to make.

As is the case with all leaders and leadership best practices, my relationship with giving and receiving respect is still a work in progress.

Since I was very young, my grandmother instilled in me the reality that I would have to work harder than others to be successful and respected. To this day, I do everything at 200 percent. I have sacrificed relationships, homes, time, money, and, to varying degrees, any notions of a personal life to make sure my company and employees succeeded. I'm most comfortable working, though. My business is my addiction, but I have had to accept that I cannot expect everyone who works for or with me to share that level of commitment and work ethic. As unbelievable as it may sound, I had to learn that someone putting in 100 percent at work was actually really good. Someone else's 100 percent, I realized, will most likely differ from my own interpretation of what "100 percent" means. Learning how to determine someone else's maximum effort and ability—which I believe can only be assessed on an individual, case-by-case basis—is critical to a leader's goals for establishing mutual respect in their relationships with others.

Stay mindful of the importance of treating yourself and others with genuine respect and care, as it makes the difference between a leader and a boss. Until you respect yourself, you cannot truly believe in yourself. If you do not believe in yourself, you cannot respect or lead others.

It's also critical to take care of yourself, regardless of your career position. If you do not care for your physical and/or mental well-being, then it's a good sign that you do not have a healthy respect for yourself.

You need to demand that others treat you with respect as well. Again, a major component of building respect for yourself and others requires stepping away from bad influences in your life. If you surround yourself with people who do not care about your physical or mental well-being, then it's usually a good sign that you don't adequately respect yourself. And allowing negative influences to control your sense of self-worth is a sure bet that you never will.

CHAPTER SEVEN

IMPLEMENTATION

n 2017, I found myself at a crossroads both in my personal life and in my role as an entrepreneur and CEO. At this point in my story, business was growing, I was in a relationship with the person I would come to think was the love of my life, and everything was moving in the right direction—for me, at least. During this time, in what ended up being our last year together, my partner lost his job and began to struggle with my hectic schedule even more than he had earlier in our relationship. I sympathized with him while making it clear that the business always had to come first.

I had learned to ignore the "noise" at home, opting instead to focus my attention on work virtually nonstop as I tried to scale my company to a larger international presence. First, we focused on expanding to the UK and then on to Barcelona, India, and Singapore. There was simply too much at stake for too many people by that point, and I believed it selfish and senseless to allow it all to take the back seat so I could have more time for my personal life. I had someone that was willing to support me, even as the "number two" in my life, but I wasn't willing to do the same for him when he needed me the most.

It was always about growing the business by any means necessary, for better and for worse at the time. One of the biggest lessons I learned was that success always comes at a price. You will have to decide for yourself what you value most and what price you're willing to pay in order to build the life and business you want. You have to ask yourself if you are willing to sacrifice and pay that price before you take the plunge into entrepreneurship, as any indecision around this necessity could jeopardize both your business and your personal life.

As I contemplated how much I was willing to sacrifice over time, I heard the words of my father, former friends, and employees telling me that I was going to fail. I realized that to be successful, I was going to have to pay the toll. Understanding to the end, my partner and I decided to split up, and because it had to be me, I moved to Barcelona to support and grow the company during its next growth phase.

Months later, I decided to take a trip to Dubrovnik, Croatia, where I rented an incredible home on a secluded island and invited a handful of friends to help me celebrate my birthday and a long-overdue vacation. I informed the staff that I would be out of the office and was trying to disconnect. Within hours of our arrival, however, I was on my phone and computer trying to catch up on the more than five hundred emails I was getting on a daily basis, a task to which I would be obligated for the majority of the trip.

My friends were initially dismayed by the degree of my workaholism. Three of the five friends I had invited were also CEOs of their own businesses, which made me feel even more concerned about the price I was paying to run my own business. Was I doing it the right way? Was there even another way at all? I wasn't sure at the time; I was just obsessed with building my company and was in overdrive constantly in order to do it.

Luckily, my friends found ample opportunities to soothe their disappointment in the blue waters of the Adriatic Sea or on the ancient streets of Dubrovnik. I, on the other hand, was forced to confront what I had known for some time now: without implementing better operations practices and creating more delegation possibilities, the leadership style I had adopted as CEO would not be sustainable for rapidly growing the company, let alone for my own physical or mental well-being. I needed to increase engagement, streamline policies and procedures where possible, and loosen the reins enough to allow new and current team members to take on more responsibilities. That trip ultimately marked the start of my shift in management style and mentality. After realizing that, hiring the right talent, setting up the right training, and making sure all parties are set up for success became key factors in taking the company to the next level.

I had formed my company on my own, and in the beginning, I had developed into the role of CEO in a somewhat self-taught fashion. I did not have a mentor to look to for customized assistance; I had to seek out the answers I needed and learn as I went along. That's the path for so many young entrepreneurs, and though we are fortunate to have such unprecedented access to a world of information at our fingertips, it can also be overwhelming at times and confusing to navigate. I soon sought the assistance of mentors, colleagues, experts, and others to help me construct a strategy for implementation in general, in order to apply the same principles as consistently as possible to the widest range of needs. The hope was to be more efficient and effective with time, to enable better agility and greater options for decision-making throughout the organization, and to be more productive overall. In other words, I needed to get *more* shit done, but I didn't want to burn myself or anyone else out trying to do it.

PEOPLE CULTURE:
IMPLEMENTING THE RIGHT PEOPLE AND POSITIONS

Any time you need to delegate tasks or implement something new within your organization—whether it be a new company policy, branding or marketing campaign, leadership strategy, market or consumer direction, or something else—you have to keep your eye on engagement among your workforce. By that I mean you will need to have a good idea how engaged people are in their work and the organization generally both before and after giving them something new that impacts them. HR work, after all, ultimately is about one thing: ensuring that the company doesn't hurt itself by doing wrong to its employees.

The primary benefit to a more engaged workforce is that it is proportionally more productive and stable, of course, but even those ideas have their roots elsewhere. A continued rise in significance from such factors as steepening global competition, technological advancement, tax legislation, and shifts in social views and realities have all contributed to a fracturing of the corporate dominance we observed in the latter part of the twentieth century. A 2015 study from the Washington, DC–based think tank the Tax Foundation found that there were one million fewer C corporations (i.e., the IRS-coded companies we typically define as a major corporation) at the time than there were at their peak in the mid-1980s prior to the Tax Reform Act of 1986. Since 1986, the Tax Foundation noted, "roughly 40,000 US corporations have disappeared from the tax rolls. However, the losses have accelerated since 2006 to a rate of about 60,000 per year."[10]

---

10   William McBride, "America's Shrinking Corporate Sector,"
     Tax Foundation, January 6, 2015, https://taxfoundation.org/
     america-s-shrinking-corporate-sector.

In the wake of the C corps' exodus, large numbers of niche-focused S corps and sole proprietorship entities have emerged, often employing just one person or a small team of employees who work to serve smaller and/or more specific markets, customer bases, and industries. As the size of so many businesses shrink and their specialties fragment, the idea of treating employees more like individuals with specialized skills is helping to drive some of the shift in the way people think about work as well as their perceptions of the companies that employ them.

Central to that shift lies in company culture, having revealed more of its influence on recruitment, engagement, production, and retention issues in recent decades. For a company culture that draws in top talent, I've learned that it's best for an organization to determine its own set of values and singular purpose, both of which need to be in accordance with the kind of people they wish to attract. Those values and sense of purpose need to be clear in all of the company's messages to define its culture clearly and to reinforce it continuously once it does.

The more I learned about engagement, the clearer the correlation between company culture and productivity became. But I also realized that engaging the workforce requires strong leadership, one that's capable of explaining clearly and consistently what's happening in the workplace and why, as more employees want to feel like they're a part of their company's evolution and progress. Perhaps most in need of being in the loop are those responsible for implementing changes throughout the organization, as they will be essential to the success of any changes made within the organization that impact the overall workplace and/or workforce culture. Because managers are actually doing the crunch work, in terms of operations, they need to understand why a particular change is going to be good for them and their department so the inevitable difficulty of implementing it is more bearable.

Above all, for any leader to engage their workers, they first have to know who their workers are. That calls for company leaders to learn a number of things about their employees, from their strengths and weaknesses to their constraints and their needs to help resolve them.

Companies can only fully engage the type of talent that is in line with their current culture, but as the societies that produce their talent progress, the company must also keep in step. And to me, therein lies much of the problem. For a company wishing to redefine its existing culture, complications with coordinating internal changes with external needs and wants create the biggest challenges. Companies often struggle to loosen the fixed structures of their past to adapt their values and purpose to an ever-evolving present, thus losing touch with the talent they most want to attract. Values like respect and trust are increasingly prioritized by employees, and like all values, they should be clear in both hiring conversations and internal and external messages to management, to customers, to clients, to employees—everything should be resonating the same message. Companies that can succeed in making their individually tailored values central to their cultural identity gain a significant engagement advantage among today's talent and consumer base.

> **FOR A COMPANY WISHING TO REDEFINE ITS EXISTING CULTURE, COMPLICATIONS WITH COORDINATING INTERNAL CHANGES WITH EXTERNAL NEEDS AND WANTS CREATE THE BIGGEST CHALLENGES.**

A customized approach to involve the worker by appealing to their working profile, working style, and personal circumstances is critical to keeping up with the changes rippling out from the moves made by large, more progressive companies such as Tesla, Netflix, Google, CarMax, Microsoft, and Adobe. When even a few of these large and influential corporations make big changes in the way they interact with their workforce or customer base, few companies and business models can afford to sit idly by and not make some changes themselves. After all, the external environment surrounding a particular industry deeply affects people both inside and outside the organization, so to attract good talent, you have to be mindful of where everyone else is too.

CREATING A VISION AND MISSION FOR YOURSELF AND OTHERS

When I first founded Elements, I had a vision for its future as one capable of competing against much larger corporations on an international stage. I saw opportunities to use certain technologies and package particular knowledge and skill sets in such a way that would make us the best option for handling a company's HR infrastructure and compliance issues anywhere in the world. I didn't know all the details around how I could do that at the time, but I knew enough to see that it was possible. I had the vision for what I wanted to create, and that, I believe, is the most important thing to have when you begin building a company or leading an existing one. You have to know where you want to go and why.

If you don't have a vision for your future and know the *why* behind your choices, then you are more likely to get lost in the storms when they come. Why? Because you haven't aligned your vision of a destination with a specific route to take you there. You can't drive to the store without knowing where it is; nor can you get what you need once you arrive without knowing why you went there in the first place. So why would you think you can reach your goals without knowing why they exist or how to get to them? Unfortunately, many entrepreneurs and CEOs tend to forget the importance of setting a vision for themselves and/or their organizations. Sometimes, the daily grind gets in the way, and being the keeper of the vision doesn't stay on the priority list. But as soon as the leader begins to lose sight of the vision of the company, so, too, will those who are following their lead. Reaffirming the vision of your company must be made a priority every day until it becomes part of the DNA of the company's culture.

Keep in mind that the company vision doesn't look at the short-term future, though. It answers what the company wants to be in the long term, say five to ten years into the future. It can be your big, hairy, audacious goal, or "BHAG," as Jim Collins and Jerry Porras put it in their groundbreaking 1994 book *Built to Last: Successful Habits of Visionary Companies*. It can be your identity as an organization, your company's unique ability, or the process your company has incorporated to generate sustainable growth. What matters is that the vision has a long-term focus and aligns with your company's mission, which centers on the company's main focus, passion, purpose, and/or cause.

The purpose of setting a vision has two parts. First, it sets a long-term course for where the company is going. Second, it aligns everyone around the company's direction and thus makes the implementation of specific policies, procedures, duties, etc. to get there easier and faster. When everyone is aligned with the vision, leaders can create unique synergies. No longer do team members guess at the direction of the company. They already know the answer, because it's repeated in some form consistently and clearly (e.g., at every annual, quarterly, monthly, and weekly meeting, in daily "huddles," during employee reviews, at team-building events). Synergy and alignment cultivate positive energy in the workplace. And positive energy leads to momentum building, which leads to maximizing efforts toward the vision's goal(s).

Teams should be informed regularly of their and their company's goal progressions, too. That way, they don't spend energy thinking about the "what ifs" or wondering where they are going. They can focus instead on actually getting to their individual destination by assessing what priorities need to be met on a daily, weekly, monthly, and/or yearly basis to achieve the company's vision.

A **vision statement** is one of the, if not *the*, best ways to communicate exactly where an individual, group, or entire organization wants to go and why. A vision statement should have the ability to inspire and motivate others around a concept or idea. It can establish a benchmark and provide line of sight, direction, and purpose, all of which the individual or organization can use to judge their actions against their core values.

Crafting a vision should establish something on the horizon that is out of our comfort zone, challenging us to stretch ourselves to our fullest potential. But it should also be something that's attainable. This allows others to invest in the future with an understanding of their purpose and role in it.

When creating my own vision statement, I learned that letting theory get in the way of reality is not always helpful. Don't get caught up in a textbook definition of a vision statement versus a mission statement either. While the mission generally refers to one's passion, purpose, and/or cause, vision focuses on these three questions:

1. What is your core focus?

2. What is your unique ability? What is your differentiator?

3. Who, what, and/or where do you want to be in five to ten years?

For instance, Google aims to "organize the world's information and make it universally accessible and useful." At Southwest Airlines, the vision is fun, distinct, and specific along three different long-term goals: "To become the world's most loved, most flown, and most profitable airline."

Each of those vision statements tells you what the organization's greatest goal is, what the organization specializes in, and where or what they aim to be as an organization in the long term.

The **mission statement** is centered on *why* your company exists. It answers the questions "What is your passion, purpose, or cause, and why is it important?" For example, the mission statement of the Alzheimer's Association is simple but powerful: "A world without Alzheimer's disease."

Knowing your mission is critical to the organization's ability to implement new ideas and processes, as you need solid alignment within the organization to envision and execute change effectively when needed. Each employee, from top to bottom, should be able to identify and articulate why they work for the company, as well as what the company is ultimately trying to accomplish.

We know people come to work with an abundance of personal issues because we all do it ourselves. Some are simply trying to pay their bills. Others are facing real crises, such as a chronic illness, a child with a disability, divorce, death. The list can go on. Whatever the personal issues may be, at some point, every employee will ask themselves, "Why am I here?" They should be able to answer that question quickly, and the answer should be something they can take at least some amount of pride in by knowing they are playing an important part in creating something valuable. If employees and volunteers at the Alzheimer's Association are asked what they do and why they do it, for example, they should be able to say something along the lines of, "Without me doing my job, a world without Alzheimer's may not happen."

The intent of your mission statement is to set an inspirational tone and mindset. It provides a purpose for the vision. Simon Sinek's TED talk and his 2009 best-selling leadership book *Start with the Why* are great examples of aligning others around your vision and mission, as Sinek asks not *what* your company does or *how* it does it but rather *why* it does it.

There are numerous examples of financially successful companies who lost their way, and a great many of them involve losing sight of one's vision and mission. Netflix's upending of Blockbuster is an example I'm sure most of us are familiar with, and it's a lesson from which we can all learn.

In the early 2000s, with Netflix already mailing out more than a million DVDs per day, Blockbuster's mission was still "to be the global leader in rentable home entertainment by providing outstanding service, selection, convenience, and value." That's a nice-sounding mission statement that's clear on what the company's long-term goals and strategies are, but it lacks focus on a bigger, more inspiring sense of purpose. On the other hand, Netflix's mission was to "entertain the world." That sounds like a simpler yet loftier mission, one that, in retrospect, indicated that Netflix's leadership had a broader, more agile vision for where and how Netflix was going to grow simply by focusing on the core *why* their business existed: entertainment.

Although Blockbuster eventually offered Netflix an acquisition deal worth $50 million that would see Netflix run the company's online business as Blockbuster.com (Netflix rejected the offer), Blockbuster never seemed to take seriously the rising popularity of video streaming until it was too late. They planned for a future in which streaming would be a small, alternative revenue stream rather than the dominant method of consuming video entertainment that it has since become. In just ten years, the failure to see farther, think bigger, and change faster leveled the multibillion-dollar juggernaut.

What I learned from my own experience trying to build a foundation on which implementation needs could rely is to aim to be more than just a business. Hold yourself to the highest standards, and while you may not be able to meet every one of them every time, you will always find ways to do better. Without the excitement of progress, purpose, and competition, complacency will take hold throughout the organization. Before you know it, you're Blockbuster, a former great company that had once been driven by innovation but fell behind rapidly because it didn't have a strong enough vision to implement the changes needed to save them from extinction fast enough. Be intentional with your vision and mission statements by ensuring that you and your leadership team truly understand them, believe in them, and live them every single day.

Vision is critical to great leadership, because to make positive change possible, leaders first need to know where they're going. The problem is that where you're going can't be determined until you know both where you currently are and exactly why you're trying to go anywhere at all. Change is hard and painful, so it must be seen as something that's so important that it overrides the temptation to stay safe and comfortable. To move an organization forward, everyone must understand, and believe in, the organization's fundamental purpose. I don't mean its day-to-day purpose of fulfilling specific tasks to meet a particular goal. I mean its philosophical purpose. To know that means going deep into the identity of the organization, and not just by asking who you are as a leader either. After all, you can't know *who* you are in that role until you know *why* you are in that role.

Everyone in the company must ask themselves why the organization exists so often that the answer is ingrained in every decision they make, large and small. Once they do, it's possible to navigate the uncertainties of change as a unified group. It's critical to align this thinking with staff, leadership, and even make sure your company's "DNA" is broadcasted consistently to those less connected to the internal workings of the company, such as suppliers, contractors, clients, and consumers.

I know what you're thinking, and you're right. It's not as easy as it sounds. Whether for yourself as an individual or for an entire organization, discovering or reaffirming a vision and mission for either one requires a great deal of reflection and a willingness to embrace some level of risk. Neither is easy, but if sustainable growth and creating alignment with others are what you're after, it's the only way to get there.

CREATING AND MAINTAINING ALIGNMENT DURING TIMES OF CHANGE

Nearly all businesses know what they do. Most companies can tell you what products and services they offer and what their target sales goals are. Some, if not many, companies can tell you how they do what they do and explain their unique ability or differential value proposition. However, it is the rare company that can tell you why they do what they do.

My experience with employees over the years has taught me that there is one common theme that runs through everyone: we all have problems, issues, or drama that we bring with us to work at some point in time. Some issues are more critical than others, but over time people's personal crises will impact their performance. I've had several eye-opening moments as a CEO where I've witnessed how events large and small in a person's nonwork life can negatively impact their job performance or spur them to begin questioning why they even show up for work in the first place. I know I can't control what happens outside of my workplace, but I do have a significant degree of control over what goes on within it. Over the years, I've come to appreciate the many ways in which that level of control enables me to provide a positive place for myself and everyone on my team to work.

To best use my ability to implement a wide variety of changes within my workplace, I knew that the true purpose of the company had to be real, it had to be understood by everyone, and our commitment to it would have to be proven consistently and sometimes boldly. Whether someone has an "off" day or is at their highest level of performance, it is crucial that they are aligned with the *why* of the organization. In times of both high-flying confidence and subterranean levels of self-doubt, knowing—and believing in—why you do what you do will keep driving you forward on the correct path. It's also what will keep a team moving toward its goals together. Having alignment around a common purpose acts as the rivets holding the plane together in times of unpredictable weather. You just won't be able to implement the changes in course you need to make en route to your destination without it.

Perhaps the most important role of the CEO is to serve as the guardian of the company's vision and mission. I suspect you have heard the expression "The company was an overnight success." In reality, no one person or company is an overnight success. Most likely, years of training, countless hours of difficult work, and many behind-the-scenes acts of dedication and sacrifice were all in motion before the success occurred. The same foundation applies to the mission and vision. If you neglect to build the foundation of unity around the vision and mission of the organization, how can anyone create alignment when it's time to implement changes?

In *Good to Great*, Jim Collins talks about the momentum of the flywheel. What he's referring to is synergy. Until you create a collective momentum in an organization, you can grow, but you won't grow to your maximum potential. You won't reach your growth potential because you aren't leveraging the full talents of the people around you. And you can't leverage anyone's full "human capital" until you implement a vision and mission they can actually buy into. The really talented people out there want great leaders who are capable of empowering them, and you can't empower people unless you are all aligned around who you are as a group, why you exist, and what you want to accomplish.

> **IF YOU NEGLECT TO BUILD THE FOUNDATION OF UNITY AROUND THE VISION AND MISSION OF THE ORGANIZATION, HOW CAN ANYONE CREATE ALIGNMENT WHEN IT'S TIME TO IMPLEMENT CHANGES?**

Perhaps the biggest key to securing alignment around the vision and mission as an organization is your ability as a leader to inspire others. Ask any successful entrepreneur or CEO if they are intentional about being an example of their company's vision and mission, and I'm willing to bet that they would say yes. I would even be willing to bet that they invest in their teams and know how to create a purpose around everything their organization does.

There are numerous examples of financially successful companies who eventually failed to innovate and implement improvements in their organization. In the end, those failures cost them more than quarterly profits; it cost them their reputation, which can be much more damaging than a temporary financial loss. That's why it is so crucial to be intentional with your vision and mission. Together, they are the standard-bearer for the organization's reputation and performance.

ALIGNING YOUR PEOPLE WITH THEIR PURPOSE

We spend a lot of time talking about alignment in the business world these days. We talk about cultural alignment, industry alignment, strategy alignment, and so on, but we don't talk so much about aligning the job with the actual person doing it. That's a major oversight, in my opinion, since the job's purpose and value is ultimately dependent on the person charged with executing it. What's more is that each position within an organization plays a part in fulfilling the company's vision, making it critical for every position to be held by employees who are properly aligned with the overall vision.

What I learned most by transitioning from a boss to a coach mentality had to do with balance. What I mean is that a great coach doesn't just know the responsibilities and purpose of each position; they know how to build players for each position. They know who to move to a particular position and why, as well as how to coach a player into being right for a position for which they have not been recruited. It took a long time and a lot of patience before I understood the importance of not only teaching a position in my company but also adapting a position to the talent I had or wanted. Nonetheless, I'm forever grateful that I did, and I'm confident that it played a major role in our success since.

When a company knows its purpose, has defined its values and culture, and has successfully established its brand and operational structure, keeping everything running in a smooth and orderly fashion has a lot to do with how well each element stays aligned with the other. To do that, you need to have a solid understanding of the jobs and the people doing them so you can identify when something is out of sync and what may be causing the dissonance.

With that thought in mind, it's common sense that by working to align your goals with the goals of others, combining your strengths to reach them together, everyone wins. Even better is the fact that the more present you are in your company and among the people within it, the more likely it is that you will gain something from every person and every job you make an effort to learn more about. Everyone has the potential to be a teacher, but it is up to you as a leader to discover what you might learn from them. Attentiveness and humility, perhaps more than anything else, will help you learn the nuances of other departments, jobs, and individuals, which in turn will guide you toward better ways of aligning each of them.

As we've touched on in earlier chapters, management strategies have been increasingly focused on employee engagement over the last several years, hoping to connect employees to their job in ways that drive productivity and performance toward positive outcomes. The trouble with purpose is that it can take a long time for someone to discover theirs. Some may find it very early in life and pursue it from the start of their education and career, but for most, it takes time to locate. That poses a number of difficulties for any leader trying to align people with a particular position in the company.

From a management perspective, it's easier to focus on strengths rather than purpose. While purpose is a great thing to look for and something that certainly excites people, you can generally discover your or someone else's sense of purpose in their work by focusing on their strengths.

When it comes to choice and aligning with one's purpose in today's interconnected world, one of your biggest responsibilities as a leader is to help employees be aware of their environment and who they are in relation to it. That's a big project. And because most companies don't want to get into deep psychology with every member of their team, leaders find it more effective to look at an employee's personality profile. That's why the implementation of tests like the DiSC profile (i.e., the evaluation of a person's dominance, influence, steadiness, and conscientiousness traits) have grown in popularity over the years: they focus on leveraging a person's strengths more efficiently.

When you know how people work best, it's much easier to enhance their strengths and bolster their sense of purpose. It's certainly not the role of a leader or manager to discover every employee's meaning of life, but customizing the components of a working profile to help them build an optimal work system is well worth the effort for everyone involved. It took me a while to understand and appreciate that fact, as I lacked the patience and experience to understand exactly how interconnected things like company culture, engagement, and alignment were to an organization's long-term sustainability. The patience and experience I've gained since then have, in my opinion, improved my ability to lead and to form stronger bonds with others in both my personal and professional life.

I had to learn almost everything about leading a business on my own, partly due to pride and my insistence on being self-reliant and partly because I lacked the support of a mentor when I started my company. But I got there because I learned that not only do you need a plan A, B, C, D, E, F, and G, you also have to be able to implement your plan. Once a plan is implemented, however, you have to hold yourself and others accountable to it.

CHAPTER EIGHT

ACCOUNTABILITY, PERCEPTION, AND TRUST

O ne of the most challenging elements of business leadership for me has been the art of maintaining accountability in the workplace while simultaneously managing my and others' perceptions. A popular expression you've likely heard before is that "perception is reality." In other words, the way someone perceives something is often the truth to them, regardless of whether it's actually true or not. The line between our perceptions and reality is where you're most likely to find trust. The narrower or more askew that line becomes, the less trust one is likely to have for a particular thing, whether it's another person, ourselves, a situation, an organization, or something else. The need to hold someone else or ourselves accountable for a particular responsibility forces all of us to reckon with our and others' perceptions and the level of trust that stems from them. But accountability should not be thought of as punishment. Accountability simply ensures that an individual or group of individuals are actually made responsible for the duties they have agreed to perform according to written and/or verbal agreements, and it's a number one priority for any organization or leader.

Early in my time as CEO, I struggled with accountability—both my own accountability and holding others accountable. I had a tendency to avoid conflict, sweep things under the rug, or even run away from problems. It took time for me (and still does at times) to mature as a person and as a leader. I had to step back and foster the courage within myself to stay committed to my plans, implement the lessons I'd learned from past mistakes, and build a team I could trust. Almost as importantly, I had to learn to trust my team so they could actually deliver on the plans we had put into motion. As a leader, you must trust yourself enough to know that you're capable of putting into place a team that can execute your plans and then give them the space to deliver. At the same time, you have to stay realistic, knowing that an accountability system will be needed in order to monitor your team's progress, identify problems, and find solutions.

KEY PERFORMANCE INDICATORS

The global pandemic brought about waves of remote work, furloughs, layoffs, transfers, and entire shutdowns. No industry was left unaffected, and more likely than not, we won't know the full impact of these disruptions for several years because many of them are ongoing. Even before COVID-19 settled into our daily lives, though, it was clear that engagement in the American workforce could be improved upon. A 2018 study by Gallup found that highly engaged teams are 21 percent more productive than disengaged teams. The main factors driving that productivity rate were that highly engaged teams had a 41 percent lower absentee rate and that they had a turnover rate 59 percent lower than disengaged teams.[11]

Of course, a myriad of other factors exists when assessing an individual's productivity. Do they understand their purpose? Could the work environment be customized to better accommodate their needs? Could the function of their job be better personalized? Is the system used to measure their performance accurate, and is it evolving in step with internal and external changes and challenges? All of these questions require thoughtful answers before companies can expect to improve their engagement numbers, and thus their productivity. Consistent and thoughtful communication with workers is vital, and the best way to secure those answers, track their progress, and assess next steps is through the use of **key performance indicators**, or **KPIs**.

Leaders generally have an intuitive nature (a.k.a. gut feelings) that allow us to make decisions based on a limited amount of data. While intuitiveness is important, it is equally important to back your decisions with analytical data. Perhaps more importantly, future decisions should be based on trending data. As you know by now, we refer to this data as KPIs, which are broken down into two categories: **leading indicators** and **lagging indicators**. Leading indicators help predict what the future may look like and can assist your ability to make proactive decisions. Lagging indicators tell you what has already happened, meaning that you make reactive decisions based on the data presented. Many of us have a tendency to allow theory to get in the way of reality. We can make things more difficult than they are, sometimes because it promotes our

---

11   Naz Beheshti, "10 Timely Statistics about the Connection between Employee Engagement and Wellness," *Forbes*, January 16, 2019, https://www.forbes.com/sites/nazbeheshti/2019/01/16/10-timely-statistics-about-the-connection-between-employee-engagement-and-wellness/.

ego or our own ideas. For that reason, let's apply the **Keep It Simple, Stupid (KISS)** principle here to keep things in perspective.

In short, the KISS principle instructs companies to first consider the most basic needs and functions of their operation, typically by focusing on three financial needs to build a sustainable business:

1. Make revenue.

2. Generate cash flow.

3. Build wealth.

In the pursuit of those three basic financial needs, however, are three components that are usually internally competing with one another within your business:

1. Revenue growth (vanity)

2. Profitability (sanity)

3. Cash (reliability)

You must create leading and lagging indicators for each of the three components in order to make proactive decisions as well as reactive ones. Eventually your intuitiveness will be rewarded through proactive decisions, or you will have to course correct based on the lagging indicators.

In the meantime, you are empowering your teams to make their decisions based on your KPIs and with the clarity and alignment of your vision and mission.

Let's explore a few points before we go further:

1. **Vanity.** Not all revenue is good revenue. For example, if you double your revenue but it has a negative impact on your company culture, your profit margins, or consumes your cash flow, are you making the right business decision? Your KPIs will help answer the question for you.

2. **Sanity.** Profitable doesn't mean you have maximized your profits. Can you increase your margins by reducing your cost of goods? Are all items you sell based on the same cost structure and same profit margin? If you produce or sell more of a specific good or service, will it reduce your overall cost? The desire is to maximize profitability. Again, your KPIs will help answer the question for you.

3. **Reliability.** Cash is king in business, hence its reliability. That means you need to do whatever you can to pad your cash reserves. Can you increase your cash flow by reducing your inventory? If you decrease your accounts payable by a specific number of days, what impact does that have on your cash flow? Once more, your KPIs will help answer the question for you.

PRODUCING A PRODUCER

Competing in the global landscape is pressing many new imperatives onto companies regardless of whether they're directly competing in international markets, but perhaps none is as urgent or as important as innovation. The need to get workers to innovate becomes more necessary as technology itself innovates and spreads, leading to more options (and therefore competition) for individuals, governments, and companies. The only way to stimulate innovation among workers, however, is not only to address creativity and collaborative techniques at the company level but also to leverage the skills and talents of every worker. Hence the importance of company culture and its emphasis on vision and mission. If a company changes the physical work environment but still treats its workers as a monolith, then they haven't actually changed the culture and won't get the most out of each worker.

That's why productivity and personalization go hand in hand. Ideally, leaders and managers would understand the strengths and weaknesses of each worker to solve productivity problems in the workplace. In that sense, engaging an employee becomes a question of how you can understand them and how to support them once you do.

ENGAGING AN EMPLOYEE BECOMES A QUESTION OF HOW YOU CAN UNDERSTAND THEM AND HOW TO SUPPORT THEM.

Certainly, job requirements change, particularly if you must work from home. It is important to create buy-in with employees; therefore, collaboration should occur between the direct report, their boss, and perhaps an additional person or group to define expectations and accountabilities.

The buy-in comes from listening to one another, with the goal of gaining insights into how you can create a productive work situation. Taking an incremental and trial-centric approach toward improving engagement helps to alleviate the anxieties of reworking familiar structures. At its core, personalizing work structures and functions is a matter of maximizing individual potential, a kind of guerrilla tactic of doing more with less, if you will.

Generally speaking, organizations should have somewhere between five and seven KPIs. Each KPI will be made up of the key lagging and leading indicators that shape where the company is coming from and where it is going. It allows the management team to recognize if someone is meeting the established expectations, and it helps them track if an individual team or person is being held accountable for meeting those expectations.

Generally speaking, the top five to seven KPIs should focus on the following areas:

1. **Revenue growth,** by total sales or specific targeted product or service unit

2. **Profitability by gross margin,** by product or service, by each division, and by net margin

3. **Cost of goods sold,** by operational costs, by departmental cost, and by targeted new products/services

4. **Cash flow,** by outstanding day receivable and outstanding day payable, inventory turns

By measuring these KPIs monthly, you are informing your team on what you believe is important to the success of the company as well as letting them know that you are monitoring it.

The second level of KPIs are senior-level indicators. Each manager should have three to five indicators that allow the CEO to see how the manager is performing. For example, if you have a manufacturing facility, you may have three KPIs that focus on the operational manager's effectiveness:

1. Production volume (i.e., number of pounds or product produced during a day/week)

2. Percentage of operating efficiency (i.e., percentage of items produced for the day/week)

3. Order accuracy shipped on time (i.e., percentage of orders shipped to customers on time)

The third level of KPIs is for each department. These KPIs should be centered on the annual goal for the year and how each department can influence that goal. For example, if the goal is to reduce cost structure of a finished product, each department should measure three things that can help meet the goal.

These leading and lagging indicators should be measured each week and each month so teams can monitor trends and pivot if necessary or make adjustments prior to facing a major issue.

ASSESSING PERFORMANCE

Once you assess ways to personalize work structures and purpose, individual performance will tell you how successful your efforts have been. There should be trial periods to any change, as you carefully monitor whether they seem to be helping an employee meet expectations. Some employees may perform worse when working from home, for instance, while others may perform better.

Monthly performance reviews may help employees be more productive by offering a constant feedback loop. Because annual reviews are backward facing in nature, they are less beneficial to an individual's development, engagement, and the company's productivity overall. Even better still is the use of weekly one-on-one meetings between managers and their direct reports to provide and discuss immediate feedback on their KPIs.

When executed well, the nature of these meetings should feel less like an interrogation and more like a conversation aimed at finding solutions to performance problems, building on successes, facilitating productivity, and reducing any stress or unhappiness employees may be feeling in the workplace. Striking a good balance in the frequency and tone of the meetings reinforces the idea to employees that their company is supporting them and actively collaborating with them to help make their work experience better. That type of regular and open communication is incredibly helpful toward empowering employees.

INCENTIVIZING PERFORMANCE

A common topic that has surfaced alongside the rise in remote workers is the issue of acknowledgment and promotion. Those who spend the most time in the office tend to be the ones who are top of mind for managers when promotions arise. It's a natural inclination to grow closer to those we physically see and interact with on a regular basis, but ensure that you compare peoples' performances rather than consciously or unconsciously saying, "Well, I've seen Gloria the most, so Gloria is up for a promotion" instead of "We see Gloria working long hours, and it seems that her dedication is deserving of a promotion."

Keep in mind, too, that different jobs track differently. That's why it's important that KPIs are thoroughly considered and discussed for each department, position, and individual. Remember, however, that even though the departmental team may be responsible for the result, the leader is accountable for the result. That's similar to how a team may be responsible for its performance, but like a coach, the leader is accountable for its wins and losses.

KPIs can change over time because customers may care about different things as time goes on and products or services evolve. You shouldn't be tracking the same things if customers aren't evaluating your products and services in the same way, so KPIs also need to adapt in parallel with those changes. The whole point is to get the most out of people, so their goals need to reflect what the project or company vision is ultimately trying to achieve.

Ultimately, having employees with enhanced skills or understanding in a particular area is something from which the company will benefit. But it also makes the individual feel like the company has listened to them, cared for them, and made them a bigger part of the company's progress mission. Not to mention that you can do something that will help them develop as a person, which does wonders for employee retention.

There's a long list of attractive add-ons that companies can utilize, but the most effective perks depend on the individual. Workers may not take advantage of everything, and you don't have to give them every bell and whistle in order to make them happy and/or more productive, but incentives are increasingly common in the battle to engage employees and improve work culture. It absolutely behooves the company to get personal with employees to understand the types of benefits they want and the types of accommodations or help they may need. Only then can you incentivize employees' performance efforts and improve their overall happiness and productivity in the workplace. Just make sure that any incentive program is directly tied to their KPIs. In the end, after all, KPIs are designed to manage the company. What isn't measured isn't managed. And in the spirit of transparency, we share the KPIs with our employees so that they feel part of the success as well as aligned with the goals we're trying to achieve.

STEPS TO CREATING PERFORMANCE TRACKING TOOLS (E.G., KPIS)

1. Meet with your management team or mentor and ask them, "What is important?" Measure what is important to them first, then look at leading and lagging indicators from financial reports to begin uncovering where the problems and critical areas of importance are. If something isn't adding value to the company, then it's usually not important. You know you have the right KPIs in place by sharing all the data interdepartmentally and working together to establish realistic goals that still push and allow for growth.

2. You will need to reevaluate your KPIs on a regular basis. As KPIs improve performance, the goalposts need to be moved, so to speak, to ensure continued progress. The fundamentals don't change, but the KPIs need to be tweaked over time. For instance, a five-person sales team has its limits even when hitting all of its KPIs. When that happens, additional salespeople may be needed. The fundamentals of how the sales team operates don't change, but the KPIs tell you that growth is needed. If you add salespeople but don't tend to your production needs, then production (e.g., research and development, packaging, distribution) is going to see a lag in its KPIs. Through KPIs you are creating transparency; through transparency you are creating clarity; through clarity you are creating alignment.

3. Less is more when it comes to KPIs. The more KPIs you have, the less significant each one will be. Pick no more than five key indicators per meeting to demonstrate the status of the company. Those indicators should be chosen according to your audience.

4. Regardless of department or audience, the organization should have five main KPIs that transcend all departments/groups. Each department or group should have three KPIs specific to them. KPIs should be relative to how you perform. Department heads oversee disseminating that information.

DELEGATION

Creating a rhythm and maintaining perpetual motion, instilling loyalty, trust, and purpose in others, defining reliable key performance indicators—all of these essential ideas depend on one important feature to how you work: delegation. Without the ability to successfully delegate responsibilities to others, no leader can sustain themselves or their organization. As I've learned personally over the years, it's simply impossible to do everything yourself, especially as the organization grows. You will only burn yourself out and/or crash the company trying.

At the same time, delegating responsibilities is one of the hardest aspects of leadership. Whether the apprehension to assign responsibilities to others stems from feelings of guilt, poor self-confidence, a lack of trust in others, or just a need to make certain that things are done to your own liking, telling others what to do and trusting that they will be able to do it is a complicated but necessary duty of every good leader.

It doesn't come naturally at first. When I recall my own experience with delegation and speak with other leaders, the reasons why I've struggled with the concept are generally similar to theirs: "So much is at stake." "The line between success and failure feels razor-thin." "Everything ultimately rests on my shoulders; I'm the person in charge of producing successful results no matter what, so I need to know everything that's going on at all times." That equation often adds up to a feeling that you should be doing everything yourself or at least be heavily involved in doing it. After all, if you feel responsible for every job's success or failure, then it's only natural that you would want to be as involved as possible in that job's

YOU MUST ALLOW OTHERS TO TAKE ON LARGE TASKS AND THEN GET OUT OF THEIR WAY SO THEY CAN TRY TO ACCOMPLISH THEM.

process. Unfortunately, that is impossible, and you must allow others to take on large tasks and then get out of their way so they can try to accomplish them without adding unhelpful stress and energy to their bandwidth by hoovering over them.

DELEGATION RESENTMENT

Once you institute a working delegation system and have everything running as well as possible in terms of shared workload, efficiency, and results, there is a potential for delegation resentment if you have not prepared for its causes. Delegation resentment occurs when a person feels that they are being insufficiently rewarded for successfully managing their responsibilities. Let's say that you have someone who is exceeding their KPIs in every category. They are meeting their goals, meeting their quotas, aligning with the core culture, and generally doing everything that's been asked of them, only to be given more responsibilities. In effect, they feel as though they are being punished for doing great work. In truth, this happens more often than leaders may like to acknowledge, and it's why it happens that is crucial to your avoiding or remedying it.

The most common reason for delegation resentment is because leaders have too many balls in the air, so to speak, and unwittingly begin over-relying on the people they know won't require much attention. Those who consistently meet or exceed their KPIs without any help can get lost in the crowd, subconsciously shuttled to the "back burner" of your priorities list by more pressing needs and concerns. The squeaky wheel gets the grease, they say, but often it's the quiet, unproblematic parts that are neglected for too long that cost you the most.

The best way to combat delegation resentment is by making sure you reward those who consistently meet their KPIs. If you only reward them with more work and responsibilities, then it's easy to see why someone may feel as though they're being punished for working hard. Promotions, bonuses, raises, extra vacation days, a better office—there are many ways to pat a high performer on the back, so to speak, to help ensure that they don't feel like their work has gone unnoticed or unappreciated. An actual pat on the back is not going to cut it. High performers, even the most reserved and quiet among them, expect to receive better opportunities in the future for their commitment to the company. The longer it takes for those opportunities to appear, the deeper their resentment may grow.

Resentment isn't the only effect of overdelegation. Sometimes the challenges of an employee with too many responsibilities and not enough help can manifest themselves not in a disengaged attitude or a notice of resignation but in poor results.

That was the case of an employee of mine whom I'll call "Jane." She was a top performer in her department, but she had a tendency to be too hard on herself. She was as motivated to perform well and please others as she was self-critical and quiet about her own needs. Then, one day seemingly out of nowhere, she submitted her notice of resignation. I had a one-on-one meeting with her to see if I could find out why. During that conversation, she told me that she had been homeless for three months, had endured multiple deaths in her extended family in a short period of time, and had a brother battling a severe case of COVID-19, among other stresses. I knew nothing about any of Jane's struggles because she had always performed well at work and never said anything to anyone about what she was experiencing outside the workplace. Fortunately, she felt comfortable enough to tell me the truth when I inquired about her reasons for wanting to leave, and we were able to make the accommodations she needed to not only continue on with us but to also improve her situation. Sometimes the only thing you need to do to build trust with someone else is listen, and luckily that was the case with Jane. Something as simple as a genuine one-on-one conversation with someone who cared about her well-being allowed her and me to create solutions for the difficult situation in which she had found herself.

Communication is key to delegating responsibilities reasonably while also making sure those new responsibilities do not cause resentment or overwhelm the employee. Defining KPIs and establishing regular times to discuss a person's responsibilities enables you to manage the delegation process with confidence, but it also gives you the opportunity to engage with people on an individual basis and discover solutions to their problems in the workplace—sometimes outside of it as well.

STEPS TO DELEGATING RESPONSIBILITIES

Deciding when and to whom you should delegate responsibilities is one of the most critical elements of great leadership. Before you decide to give someone more responsibilities, though, you need to make sure they will be properly supported, monitored, and rewarded (either at the time of delegation or later, as long as a path to a reward has been established) in their new role. To help meet those aims, ask the following questions and ensure that these steps have been implemented prior to delegating more responsibilities to them:

1. Are they proactive in asking for more?

2. Are they willing to "own" those responsibilities?

3. Did they deliver on what they said they were going to do?

4. Are the responsibilities clearly defined, and do you have KPIs in place for the position?

5. Will they have regular one-on-one meetings with their direct boss to discuss the KPIs and assess the challenges and successes of their work?

In the end, you must realize that your main purpose as a leader is to ensure and protect the chances for your team's success. At the same time, you cannot swoop in any time there's trouble like you're Superman and start trying to fix it all, as you will likely anger and alienate your employees and/or other managers. You should maintain clear and frequent communication to express expectations, missed goals/accomplishments, warnings, problems and solutions, etc. while also providing the room for people to meet their goals and improve upon areas where needed. I know that I'm humbler now than I was when I started my business, but I'm still learning a lot about patience and trust. I understand that trust is earned both ways. I also know that it is, at a certain point, a leap of faith. But I still struggled to respond to mistakes in an agile way. I was still too hard on myself and others after I or they made a mistake, which ultimately hindered my ability to respond to it in the most effective way possible. My foray into finding outside investors for the company would prove to be my greatest test of patience and trust yet.

CHAPTER NINE

DUE DILIGENCE (AND SETBACKS)

A fter nearly six years in the making, Elements Global Services is the largest it's ever been and continues to grow in terms of employee size, client base, and international footprint. As of this writing, we have 250 internal employees, operating in more than 152 countries, fourteen regional office locations in 11 countries, and more than 30 countries with remote staff around the world and counting. Though I had dreamed of it, it's an achievement even I doubted would come to fruition this quickly, if at all, at the onset of my entrepreneurial journey.

As much as I've learned over the course of that journey, though, I'm still learning something new about leading a business on a daily basis. The job you have as a business leader is to make decisions— really hard decisions—every single day. That's what you do. It's not necessarily that you're wading through the minutiae of task work all day but rather that you are constantly strategizing, instructing, directing, and managing problems.

Just months before the pandemic forced the world into lockdown, I had made the decision to start to talk to and later bring on outside investors for Elements through a venture capital deal. As a result, my role as CEO elevated from something of a one-man-band type of boss to a leader with a board of directors to help make decisions pertaining to scaling, operations, and organizational management. The changes also came with a lot of anxiety, having to make two major pivots almost simultaneously as a young leader: first by adjusting to the venture capital world and the conditions that come with it, followed by a global pandemic that changed countless things about the way we all live and work. Handling the pivots in your trajectory and managing crises are part of the job, but so much change and so many challenges occurring so closely together was threatening the confidence I had as a leader in a major way. I had no choice, however, but to suck it up, put on my big boy pants, and reinvigorate the mindset of self-reliance, ambition, and work ethic that I've had since I was fifteen years old and get shit done. In times of unimaginable crisis, all you can do is try to survive without losing yourself or what's most important to you.

IN TIMES OF UNIMAGINABLE CRISIS, ALL YOU CAN DO IS TRY TO SURVIVE WITHOUT LOSING YOURSELF OR WHAT'S MOST IMPORTANT TO YOU.

When investors come in, even small minority investors, you have a duty to perform for them. That's one of the biggest fears for any business leader: the financial cost of someone believing in you. That fear, though, can also serve as fuel for your drive and determination to improve your business, not to mention the encouraging feeling of having someone else believe in you and your business enough to invest their own money into you and it. But it comes with additional responsibilities, particularly in regard to taking your leadership skills to new levels.

A popular expression is that a good leader spends their day working *on* the business as opposed to working *in* the business. That's true, but it's not easy getting into a position where you can step back and focus your attention on the bigger picture, especially in a new business with less capital, structure, and fewer staff to make your job easier (e.g., expanding your workforce to enable better delegation opportunities, improving your operations systems, increasing budgets for marketing and sales).

Regardless of the size or financial security of a company, though, the leader can and should still evaluate the business as a global entity (i.e., their organization and its market and industry, as well as any organizations, markets, or industries that "touch" or impact the leader's organization). A good leader needs to figure out how to take the entity from where it is to where they know it can be or where it must be in order to survive. The real challenge, though, is that the leader has to be correct in their speculations and strategies, or they may not have anything to lead at all.

Making predictions about, and executing plans for, the future of your organization and the environment it inhabits is a challenge that will require both focus and perseverance. It demands a lot of due diligence as well—that is, assessing the risks and benefits of a particular business or decisions that will impact that business. These decisions dictate the direction, and fate, of the company, and they fall directly on its leadership. When you're wrong, lives change because of it. People may lose their jobs, bills may not be paid, growth may stall or regress, and lawsuits may even be filed. That's what makes due diligence so important. It's critical toward making sound decisions that you'll be less likely to regret later. In that way, not only is due diligence necessary for the success of your business decisions; it's also necessary for maintaining good mental health during your entrepreneurial ride.

The weight of your decisions as a leader is heavy, and it will likely get heavier as the company grows. Like most of us I suspect, stress became a constant fixture in my life during the early stages of the pandemic. I made a pledge to my employees that there would not be any COVID-19 terminations. Then I flew from Spain—where I was living and working in our Barcelona office—to the United States to work with our US-based offices, only to be stranded in Washington, DC, from March to November of 2020 in a corporate apartment. I had trouble eating and sleeping normally. I could only watch movies or television shows set in some alternate reality far away from my own.

Maintaining a positive mindset in the face of relentless uncertainty about your life and business is a vital element to any entrepreneur's success. In fact, that "can-do" attitude we've all heard about is the defining character component of successful entrepreneurs. But I was terrified and stressed for so many reasons beyond the normal business-related ups and downs, as I imagine almost everyone was both inside and outside of our company. Still, you will never meet an accomplished entrepreneur who is also a pessimist, and I was determined to lead us through what was likely (and hopefully) the darkest, most uncertain period of time we'll face in my lifetime.

I know that anyone who sees the worst in everything and concentrates on the problems in lieu of the potential solutions will not last very long as an entrepreneur, and this was going to be a test of resolve like no other I had ever faced. Bad times will come, disasters will find you, and when they do, it's your mental fortitude that will either pull you out or bury you there.

So why are some people able to overcome stress, or even thrive under it, while it debilitates others? While there are obviously many factors unique to the individual in question, the primary reason in my own experience has been focus. What we focus on comes to define our sense of what's possible. Our ability to solve problems, build relationships, motivate others, and think clearly has everything to do with how we're able to frame the situations in front of us. Successful entrepreneurs are masters of directing their attention to what they want and how to get it while at the same time blocking out the negative thoughts that creep into one's mind when faced with challenges. Entrepreneurs must constantly reroute their mental focus back toward their goals, even though doubt, fear, and distraction will endlessly attempt to force them off course.

There are a number of tricks and concepts that I've applied to my own life and career that have helped me maintain the focus and drive I need to power me and the business through times of difficulty. If, and when, you find yourself feeling lost, disillusioned, or discouraged for any reason, try walking yourself through some of these techniques:

- Train your mind to focus unwaveringly on what you *can* control or change; what you can't control or change is a waste of both time and energy.

- Remind yourself that failures and challenges are part of the process. Look for the lesson you gained from them rather than focusing on what you might have lost, even if the only lesson is that what you tried didn't work.

- Be a beacon of hope in your organization by utilizing self-talk to stay positive and optimistic in trying times.

- Celebrate every victory no matter how small. It reinforces your confidence in facing future challenges.

CULTIVATING YOUR ENVIRONMENT:
SHOULD IT STAY, OR SHOULD IT GO?

Once I partnered with an investor, I had to do a lot of due diligence on the future of Elements. I had to create a board and appoint its directors, and I had to find ways to streamline operations and improve the structure of our company in a number of ways due to our global reach and growing size across so many different countries. One of the first things I began to focus on was the overall environment of our company, as I wanted to create a unified and consistent culture for our teams no matter where they were located in the world or what their particular role was. Enriching the work environment is a multifaceted process, one that ties culture, workplace flexibility, personalization, incentives, and so many more elements together in hopes of creating a healthier habitat in which a company can grow stronger.

As a leader, you should also keep in mind that there are many things about traditional corporate-based structures that people don't want to change, and some simply can't change even if they did. Companies cannot go backward, and no leader wants to intentionally shrink their company and send their workers to the unemployment line.

There's obviously a lot of good things that a well-managed corporate structure can offer workers. It can offer great pay and benefits, job stability, clear directives to follow, and fluid channels to ascend through if well-defined goals are reached. But knowing which elements of old to keep and which elements of new to adopt requires a lot of due diligence and some trial and error before a company gets the lush work environment it may be hoping for.

What can change most easily? You can start by identifying what people want and don't want from their work. For example, even before the COVID pandemic, many workers did not want to be in an office building working fifty or sixty hours a week if they didn't have to. Some, however, did find working in a dedicated company office to be more productive and conducive to their lifestyle or mindset. In either case, taking advantage of available technologies to make lives more enjoyable, safer, and work more productive is a no-brainer if the work itself allows for it.

Companies can also improve their work environment by adhering to rather simple principles. Managers and leaders who succeed in recognizing and respecting employees at an individual level can amend their policies and build fuller, more interactive relationships that yield greater reciprocity. Companies run because of people, and the best leaders not only know that, but they build their environment around it.

Jobs aren't as permanent as they once were, either, so cultivating a people-centric environment is especially difficult if many of them will only remain temporarily. If you're not being treated in a familial way, there's a lot of instability and disengagement from the work and/ or organization. You find nearly 100 percent of your purpose in your connection to the individual work when the organizational environment is bad. That's one reason why so many organizations today are trying to change the overall mindset in the workplace, to give workers more to connect to in their work.

Adding an outside investor and a board of directors into the mix preceding the pandemic by only a few months forced me to work even harder on implementing new policies and improving existing ones, which is a difficult process for any CEO or entrepreneur to do and especially challenging during a time of so much uncertainty and change occurring outside the workplace.

I knew that top-down and blanket policies rarely work. Internal policies need to be thoroughly thought out and executed in a way that is consistent with the organization's existing and/or desired culture as well as the needs of the workforce. Policies need to be flexible, and people and frameworks need to be able to adapt within them. Leaders, in turn, also need to be capable of setting the example to follow.

The CEO of Aetna offers us an example of beneficial policy making. After having a terrible ski accident in 2004, Mark Bertolini spent roughly a year out of the office as he fought to recover his mobility. He received expert medical care, but he also felt that homeopathic techniques, yoga, and meditation helped him reach a faster and fuller recovery than doctors had anticipated. When he returned to work, he brought in yoga and meditation for everybody. While only 28 percent of workers actually took any of the classes, it was so sufficient in reducing stress and increasing wellness among workers that it decreased the company's healthcare costs by nearly $7 million.

In the United States, the private sector is the main driver of many government policies, so it's left up to the private sector to do many things relating to work-related changes. The government, for example, does not have to step in and make parental leave mandatory in the corporate private sector if the corporate private sector keeps moving toward that idea, as it seems to be.

On the private sector side of things, however, policies need to change. Without good policy making and implementation, things like a strong work environment, increased productivity, better efficiency, and an overall good company culture can't exist. None of their benefits can come into the organization until policies are reworked and reinforced, which of course begins with due diligence around what is needed and desired within a specific company.

One issue in the way of policy making for companies is that there is a lack of reliable numbers to measure with. The Bureau of Labor Statistics is not actually gathering the statistics in a way that measures some pivotal points affecting the workplace and the workforce generally. For example, how the BLS counts the employed or part-time employees is a source of controversy. If they count a freelance worker during a week when they're not working or don't have a project, they're counted as unemployed. Some labor experts have argued that they're not asking the right questions to report accurate freelancer numbers and employment numbers overall. If skepticism surrounds the accuracy of basic labor statistics, it's hard to draw conclusions about what policies you should implement within your own organization.

Employment as a concept was classified in the early 1900s by economist John Maynard Keynes as every able-bodied man that was working full-time. Today, however, the gig economy is pushing toward a type of employment concept in which everyone is able to work as much as they need. That could be, for some people, twenty hours a week, and it could be forty or more hours a week for others. But working full time isn't the objective for everyone. In fact, it likely won't even be possible when automation hits the labor force with more impact.

From pandemics to recessions to large generational and technological changes, so many things are changing in the marketplace that virtually all of its pillars are feeling it. That, clearly, complicates policy making in the present. Leaders have to be thinking about their organization's work, labor, the general workforce and who's in it, company culture, legal, finance, health, and public perception all at once. The question is, are we tracking the right things? If not, then doing your due diligence with regard to policy making is extremely difficult.

Will the workweek go down to, say, a thirty-hour workweek? Mexican billionaire Carlos Slim believes it should, arguing that when automation strikes even harder there will be fewer hours of work to be shared among the same number of people. And when we look at GDP progress, it has always been measured by output. If we are increasing progress, then increasing output is a good thing.

WE ARE SEEING MORE AND MORE PEOPLE IN NEARLY EVERY FIELD AND INDUSTRY INCREASINGLY ASK, "SHOULDN'T WE CONSIDER OUR QUALITY OF LIFE AND QUALITY OF ENVIRONMENT AS A MEASURE OF SUCCESS, NOT JUST VOLUME OF OUTPUT?"

There is now discussion and a reevaluation of that metric, too, however, as researchers seek to understand if output should be the most important end goal. Because things like natural resources and human capital obviously have limits, there has been a shift toward conservation and stronger "people-centric policy," which is now an underlying tone in many of the policies we see facing the "future of work" conversation.

Output as a metric for success has shaped much of the private sector's mindset and thus environment, but we are seeing more and more people in nearly every field and industry increasingly ask, "Shouldn't we consider our quality of life and quality of environment as a measure of success, not just volume of output?"

As that mindset shifts, the policies we can use to meet them will need to be thought through carefully to realize their benefits and ensure that they can be enforced. The quality of life and the quality of your company's work environment should be included in those discussions and tied into those policies. Inform yourself and stay aware of all the changes taking place in the business ecosystem. Some of these decisions and findings will impact you as an employer more than others, but effective policies depend upon good information and foresight to guide them. Mindset should genuinely adapt to changes; policies should reflect that pairing and project the different possibilities of your company. The work environment and culture thrive when you do.

As I dug deeper into my own company's policies and began considering better ways that we could keep everything running smoothly and everyone on the same page as we grew, I kept coming back to these main points when brainstorming policies:

- Work to match policies to company culture.

- The pulse of the company should inform your policy.

- Open communication among employees and leaders is key to keeping tabs on the pulse of a company.

- Mindset is the "thinking culture" of a company.

- Mindset needs to be coherent throughout the company.

- Policies need to be consistent with mindset and implemented consistently and thoroughly while recognizing the evolution of the company, government, law, and society at large.

Nondisclosure agreements and nondisparagement clauses in employee contracts became an unfortunate reality for me as well, as I realized that no matter what I do or how well I do it, some people will be dissatisfied with my organization and/or with me as a leader. Even if you do everything right as a CEO or business owner, you will also have to manage the reality that you simply cannot make everyone happy all the time. Prioritize being fair and transparent with your team, but also understand that you have a responsibility to the entire company, not just to single individuals. That's a difficult reality to accept for young entrepreneurs and business leaders, but it's a critically important truth to accept. The sooner you do, the better it will be for everyone involved.

CHAPTER TEN

WHAT I'VE LEARNED AS A CEO, AND WHAT I'M STILL LEARNING

A s I have said throughout this book, there is no end point to being a good leader. A good leader learns something every day that makes them a better leader. They read; they watch videos; they speak with mentors, colleagues, and a variety of experts; and above all, they self-reflect regularly to gauge where they're coming from, where they are, and where they're going or want to go.

I was in my midtwenties when my entrepreneurial journey began, but there is no age requirement for when you can, or even should, begin or end your own journey. I have learned more about who and what I am over the last decade than perhaps I have in all of my thirty-four years combined, but I know fully well that I still have so much more to learn about myself. I've learned that I am a perfectionist, sometimes to a fault. I've learned that I put 200 percent into everything I do because I've always had to in order to succeed, and sometimes that leads to conflict with others as our expectations don't always align. But I wouldn't change any of it. Starting a business from scratch by yourself is a tremendously difficult feat, but it's equally fulfilling in ways I never imagined. As a CEO, I now see myself as a vessel for how to help people not make the same mistakes I made. That's a reward worth all the struggles I've had to overcome and then some.

Throughout my life, I have been drawn to those with ambition, a strong work ethic, and good leadership qualities. The more I saw of their success, the more I wanted for myself. That aspiration turned into a desire to achieve bigger and bigger goals, which inevitably overshadowed the fears and doubts I had to some degree. The fear was still there, but the desire to achieve what I saw made me fearless enough to pursue my own ambitions.

Let me be clear: the fear never goes away completely. I wake up with some degree of fear nearly every morning and go to sleep with some amount of anxiety too. Fear and anxiety are like cousins that way. They go hand in hand together everywhere, and they stay in whatever area of your life for however long you let them. The fears I face every morning come from two places: the fear of the unknown and the fear of loss. Not knowing what the next move is, or not knowing if I'm getting into a reliable business deal or not, is a great source of fear and anxiety in my professional life.

LET ME BE CLEAR: THE FEAR NEVER GOES AWAY COMPLETELY.

After I attained a fair amount of wealth and business success, the fear of loss became another formidable psychological opponent. When you achieve great success, you obviously don't want to lose what you have worked so hard to gain, and that desire to hold on to what you have built can become a crippling source of fear if you are not careful and begin to value the material things in your life too much.

The bottom line is that you will always have fears of one kind or another, but you will get better at managing your fear with each occasion in which you face it down.

There is a story in the Bible in which Paul mentions a "thorn in his flesh." Don't worry—I'm not going to preach to you. But I sometimes wonder what Paul might have meant by having a thorn in his side. There are many interpretations over what he might have meant, but I often return to one interpretation in particular: that the thorn was to keep him reminded of where he came from, that he was still mortal. In other words, the proverbial thorn in your flesh—fear and anxiety in this case—keeps you humble. It reminds you that you're alive but that you are not invulnerable. That fear and anxiety will likely never go away completely. If it does, it may not be such a good thing. Fear means that you still care. It keeps you sharp and engaged, but the question is how you will handle it. For me, I know that I have to tackle it head on; otherwise, it will become a debilitating problem that distracts from my work and my ability to focus on solving problems.

Fear is like a bully in school. You can't run from that bully forever, because they're going to keep harassing you. Even when you call on your teachers to help you, eventually that bully is going to find you when the teachers aren't around and mess with you even more. It's the same thing with fear. The harder you try to run away from it, the worse it gets. How do you overcome it? You have to stand and face it directly.

The best weapon I have found against fear is knowledge. Whether it be related to an individual or a company, finance, a business concept that's foreign to me, the law, or something else, I try to do as much homework on it as I can until I feel more comfortable. Knowledge is confidence, and while confidence may not be the complete absence of fear, it certainly helps to control it.

There's a great acronym that says FEAR stands for **F**alse **E**vidence **A**ppearing **R**eal. Fear of the unknown really just boils down to knowing too little about the situation. That's why so many of us often find ourselves feeling anxious about our future, because it's ultimately a complete unknown. The fear of loss that so many of us have is also a fear of the unknown, of what may happen that causes us to lose something of great value to us, whether it's a relationship or a loved one, an important opportunity, our health, our business, money, possessions, etc. When false evidence about what may happen, or perhaps even has happened, appears real to us, it's virtually impossible to come up with a viable solution to the dilemma. Fear stalls our progress by clouding our judgment and leading us off our path to the successes for which we're striving.

When I find myself in a business situation that becomes excessively stressful, I know that I have to take a break and give myself time to think long and hard about it first. I have been in situations before where someone told me, "Hey, you have to do this now because the opportunity might get away from you if you don't act quickly." As a result of believing them, I made hasty decisions that in turn caused harm to either my business or my personal life. I came to learn that I have to be a little more patient. I have to analyze the situation thoroughly and get as much information as possible so I can make a sound decision. A lot of that patience comes with experience and maturity, and rarely do you avoid the pain of the impulsivity and impatience of your youth. That's not necessarily a bad thing, either, as the pain helps you discover what *not* to do again. Above all, though, do not let others pressure you into making a decision you are not comfortable with. That's a tactic usually employed to serve their interests, not yours.

Successful entrepreneurs are not fearless; they just know how to manage it and use it to their advantage. They know how to harness their fear and let it drive them toward doing the things they need to do to get more comfortable with the situation at hand. That's one of the major factors that distinguishes successful entrepreneurs from unsuccessful ones. The successful ones do their homework. They become knowledgeable about the things that they aren't knowledgeable about, turning their weak points into strengths in order to make better, more calculated decisions. But the fear is still there. That's why we call it a calculated risk. But fear cannot be what prevents you from taking a risk and jumping on an opportunity. Instead, it should be your guide for how and when and where to jump. Courage is not something that exists in people who do not feel fear; it's a trait of those who are able to push past it in pursuit of their dreams.

Regret is another major obstacle in your pursuit of opportunity. In fact, regret can be worse than fear, in my opinion. As I have said before, fear can be used for good purposes. It can be the fuel you need to chase down an opportunity or overcome a difficult hurdle in your life or career, and it can be the warning you need to avoid bad situations. Regret, on the other hand, serves no real positive purpose to you. What's worse is that regret is hard to overcome, because it constantly pulls you back into feelings of self-doubt, self-loathing, and/or self-pity, all of which make it very difficult to use fear to your advantage. If you're eternally stuck in the past, then there's no room to think about the here and now, and certainly no room to plan for the future, regardless of your fears. You can't let regret stick to you. If you try something—let's say a business deal—and it doesn't work out, just chalk it up as a learning experience and move on. When regret is allowed to sit on top of fear, it's impossible to put fear to work for you, and it just compounds until it's a very unhealthy burden. Release the regret, and then you can use your fear to propel you forward.

ENTREPRENEURSHIP AND LEADERSHIP IN A DIGITAL WORLD

Before the Information Age, the era in which we live today, it was more difficult to access the level of opportunity that we see today. Technology is the driving force behind that ease of access to just about anything at any time, for better and for worse. For people like my parents and grandparents, especially given the era in which they grew up, it was much harder for them to get out of their situations because the opportunities for doing so were extremely limited. But today, with the global economy, and with technology connecting so many of us to it simultaneously, success has more to do with your ability to identify the right opportunities and your commitment to pursuing them.

Many of the opportunities and tools needed for your success as an entrepreneur can be found online these days. While attending business lectures and courses has certainly helped me along the way, I have learned a lot about entrepreneurship and business through my research on the internet and from books. You search for answers to virtually any question you have and find a vast sea of information on concepts, laws, tactics, tools, and more. It's the ultimate resource for gaining knowledge quickly, though you do have to be vigilant about the varying qualities of sources. With millions of individuals putting content out, it's incredibly easy to find information on nearly anything and everything. But the key is knowing how to discern whether the information is applicable to you, whether it's accurate, and how you can absorb the information and make it useful to your needs.

Years ago, technology was a component of business, but today technology drives business. That doesn't mean you have to be a technologist. You don't have to go out and get a degree in information technology or even become a technology geek to utilize its benefits. With the advancements in the technology sector over the last decade alone, tech is easier to understand and use than ever. What's most important is that you know how to leverage technology toward achieving your business goals. For example, I'm not a certified public accountant, or CPA. I didn't go to school to get a degree in business finance. But through the power of computer software and digital tools (e.g., QuickBooks, apps), small business owners are able to manage the financial aspects of their business without having to hire an entire finance team. I have accountants and other staff members review all of our financial information and report it to the appropriate authorities, but in terms of bookkeeping for a small business, modern technology can do much of it for you.

Within the last two decades, dozens upon dozens of companies went out and developed virtual businesses that now support other businesses with virtual services, such as receptionists, accountants, data entry specialists, content writers, and more. When I talk about the power of technology, I'm talking about leveraging the strength of technology to carry more of your organization's work and financial load. It's never been easier to do that than now, and it's been a huge help to a young entrepreneur like me who had to build his company largely on his own.

The structure of a business is evolving today as well, and it's largely due to technology. Over the last several years, small companies have become increasingly agile, to the point that they can be threats to larger businesses. Now larger businesses are incorporating some of the same tactics as small businesses in order to become more agile themselves. I'm sure you've heard the story of the *Titanic*, that massive and "unsinkable" ship that did just that when it crashed into an iceberg in the Northern Atlantic in 1912. One of the main reasons the *Titanic* went down was because it was too big. The crew couldn't navigate the mammoth vessel away from the approaching threat. The same can be said now for big businesses. Companies understand that they have to be nimbler, because things change so quickly, and in today's tech-driven world, virtually anyone can be a competitor.

Another excellent way to leverage technology to serve your entrepreneurial goals is to use it as a means of raising capital through consulting. You can use your skills as an individual or a company to bring more value to your business simply by selling those skills and services out to others. We often look at money as a barometer for success, but the reality is that we all will encounter situations where we lose money. But you won't so easily lose your skills. Whether you are a freelancer, independent contractor, or gig worker, today's technology gives you ample opportunities to sell your skill set to others, and you would be very wise to take advantage of that accessibility in order to either raise or save capital, or both.

Technology brings plenty of challenges along with its benefits, too, of course. The prospect of losing the comforts of permanent or periodic stillness to a mindset in which stability is constantly in motion doesn't come quietly. When people implicitly recognize that we're moving toward a very dynamic situation and will likely be losing a set of circumstances that we are comfortable with, we can expect that denial and panic won't be far behind.

People talk about a "digital transformation" a lot more today than they used to, perhaps even more than they did during the dot-com bubble. People are engaging with technology more now, and conversations always grow louder when more voices attach to them. Some of those voices say that this is a total digital transformation, a sci-fi-esque genesis in which people and businesses will forever be changed once digital technology sweeps across every aspect of human civilization. Others see it as a time to invest and cash in on the action, a kind of gold rush, but with apps and tablets instead of pans and sluice boxes. Others believe this is all just a passing trend, and we'll move on once the next big innovation comes along or perhaps even step back from our digital worlds in a kind of tech regression toward the nostalgia of a supposedly simpler time.

For me, though, the expansion of choice and the dynamics of a connected world is somewhere in between. Digital technology may not be the most important business tool of our time, but it's certainly a more important development than the time Betamax met the VCR. Like most, I see the digital elements as the drivers behind so much of the change we're seeing in society and business today, but we will still be very much the same when the dust settles. The question before us now, however, is how and where a company starts to incorporate and integrate both the technology and the ideas that come with it. The answers are a fundamental requirement if one is going to continue to be an integrated part of the modern world.

Perhaps we can examine this crossroads with a little physics. Inertia is a compelling concept when it comes to change. Let's remember that momentum is mass times velocity, so if you have a big company, the effort required to get a static giant moving is huge. The larger the company, the more effort is required to make changes to accommodate our growing number of choices (and challenges) in the way we work. Keep in mind, too, that stagnation is a choice, although it sometimes feels more like an inability to move than a decision to stay still. But in this case, the decision to act must be made, and that decision should be recognized and understood by all so that companies and the people connected to them are aware of the future path that they've decided upon.

A company should be able to communicate to everyone what the decision to act fully means. There will be many options now and many elements later on that will all be changing rapidly. Directions and decisions are required for each. They don't necessarily need to be done at the same time, as many are interdependent, but they will require thoughtful decisions and regular tracking and updating. That's why due diligence is so important to your decisions, whether they be related to internal policy, sales, client relations, human resources, or anything else involving the organization's future.

To utilize the newly afforded powers of choice in the best ways, leaders have to understand all the different places that it touches. Those in leadership have to thoroughly examine the pieces that have to do with culture, workplace flexibility, engagement, collaboration, gauging the workforce, and the employment framework in general. All of these elements are part and parcel of different things that form the whole of the company and its customer base.

Drastic changes may be necessary as new developments arise, whether they're new, tech-enabled choices that spring up or the mindsets that come along with them. How well you're going to lead them will depend on how well you track and adjust to changes attached to choice. The kind of policies you have, what your values are, how you're going to deal with change—all of these different decisions will need to be prioritized.

To be successful in leadership, I've learned, you also need to be able to identify the habits that are no longer conducive to the current environment and ensure that they aren't included in any future decisions. That can be done by taking a particular principle or idea and testing against it in the current landscape. Once you have a good understanding of the results, you should choose the principles that worked and seem likely to be useful in the future to include in your decision-making process going forward. Choosing a structure that is going to be very fixed does not work now, and I don't suspect that it will work any better in the future either. You will need a framework that allows you to pivot quickly when making decisions or adapting to changes, or you may find yourself and/or your organization stuck with old habits that can't propel you upward in growth.

EMPLOYEE PURPOSE:
TOO MANY CHOICES, TOO LITTLE TIME

As we've touched on in earlier chapters, management strategies have begun to tinker with the idea of engaging employee purpose over the last decade or so. There has also been a strong movement toward purposeful business. If you think about books like 2013's *Conscious Capitalism*, by John Mackey and Rajendra Sisodia, or the movement around the so-called evergreen companies (which design themselves to remain independent for many years) and triple-bottom line (or 3L) companies (which use a three-part accounting framework to measure the social, environmental, and financial impacts of the company), it's clear that many incredible things are happening in the ways businesses interact with society itself. At their center, ideas and actions like these are all very exciting manifestations of purposefulness.

That's great, but it's harder to get these practices into the mainstream because they are, well, "squishy." Ideas like purposefulness, social responsibility, full-cost accounting, and so forth don't directly tie to the bottom line, at least not in a way that's immediately observable. In business school—and even for those who don't go to business school—people often hear that the purpose of business is to maximize shareholder value or shareholder wealth. It's that simple, really. According to traditional views on business, the entire purpose of the company is inward facing, focusing more on putting and keeping things *in* as opposed to thinking too much about what it's putting or keeping *out*.

Another problem is that it can take a long time for someone to find what their purpose is. In those cases, I've learned rather recently that it can be easier for a leader to focus on an individual's strengths rather than on their purpose. While purpose is a great thing to look for and something that really drives and engages people in their work and life, if you can focus on someone's strengths, purpose can be found more quickly. We're moving away from the idea that management should help employees strengthen their weaknesses. Many companies are now seeking ways to "outsource" employee weaknesses and work to improve on their strengths instead.

Most of the time, if you really enjoy doing something, you'll get good at it. Sometimes people are very good at something and they can get paid well for it, but they really enjoy doing something else more. With today's increasingly collaborative and choice-friendly work environment, it's easier for people to do both. Practically speaking, that's beneficial in managing a person who's either younger and doesn't have that much experience or someone who's older and never had as many choices in their career.

But the availability of choice for employees is not without its drawbacks either. Whether employees know their purpose or not, many struggle to navigate the wide range of choices now available to them. Helping them make choices is yet another aspect of good leadership, as well as one of the most challenging. For a number of reasons, it's too difficult to dig into the deep psychology of everyone, and that's why I suggest using tools like the DiSC profile and PI to help identify their strengths and weakness in a work-related capacity and then focusing on ways to leverage those strengths more efficiently. Do they want the typical nine-to-five, forty-hour, five-day workweek in the office? Or do they want something less conventional, such as working two days a week from home or perhaps even ten-hour days for a four-day workweek? Do they perform better when they work independently, or do they thrive in a group environment? Are they a morning or an evening person? When do they work best? Working with employees to customize their working profile helps all parties better understand their working style, which helps them and/or their managers make choices around their role within the company.

When you know how people work best, it's much easier to enhance their strengths and bolster their sense of purpose. It's certainly not the role of a manager to discover every employee's meaning of life, of course. But customizing the components of a working profile to help them build an optimal work system is well worth the effort for all involved. It gets them to a place where they'll be more engaged in their work, less distracted and stressed by their challenges, and just happier and more productive overall in the work they do day in and day out.

THE CONSISTENCY OF CHANGE

With the choices that have become available and the change that people are seeing, there's a desire to take wide-ranging choice on board and recognize it as a new constant among many management strategists. The prospect of constant change without any anticipation of it letting up is something that people are frightened by. And that's an understandable fear. This is not just a hurdle to get over after all; it's a mental shift in how we view nearly every aspect of how people work.

We have talked about a wide range of personal traits and professional concepts to exercise, including patience, potential fear, regret, courage, respect, implementation, accountability, trust, the importance of doing your due diligence before making decisions, and more. Ironically, the one constant throughout all of those topics is the presence of change. Evolution is inevitable in business. You must recognize that change will have to be confronted and that it's best to do it sooner rather than later.

EVOLUTION IS INEVITABLE IN BUSINESS. YOU MUST RECOGNIZE THAT CHANGE WILL HAVE TO BE CONFRONTED AND THAT IT'S BEST TO DO IT SOONER RATHER THAN LATER.

As you, your company, or your employees prepare to navigate dramatic changes, understand that no one can adapt to them or implement them superficially. If there's nothing at the core of your choices, then you will likely be led astray and make the wrong decisions. You must be aware of your ground principles and core values, as they give you something that holds true when the landscape changes and you need a beacon to help center yourself or others.

Evaluate and prioritize the key fundamental drivers of your company. Who are the groups performing the best? Who are the influencers of those groups? Which division might be the most influential? Make sure those drivers, whether they're divisions, groups, or individuals, are on board first. They can be the ones helping the rest of the organization take these changes on board.

Above all, you have to remember that life promises trials and tribulations no matter what. The difficult times will pass, and in the end, you will be left with the choice to either lose to your mistakes or learn from them. Remember this during the lows *and* the highs, as it's just as easy to wander from the path during the good times as it is during the bad times. Anyone who puts their mind to understanding the sacrifices that will be required to be a CEO or business owner can do it. It's a lot of work and it's emotionally hard, but it's worth it in the end. For me, it's worth it because of the fulfillment I get from being able to help other people and getting to create something that helps people that didn't exist before. That excites me, and more importantly, it fills me with a sense of accomplishment and purpose.

I still struggle to rise above failures at times, but it does get easier the more you do it. The key, at least for me, has been to train myself to let mistakes be lessons rather than losses. You must have faith in the people you have tasked with a responsibility, and the only way to do that is to first have faith in yourself and your ability to lead. If I've learned anything over the last few years in particular, it's that even in times of crisis and despair, if you learn something and keep going, you can never lose as long as you continue to get shit done!

To be continued.